Palgrave Studies in Maritime Economics

Palgrave Studies in Maritime Economics is a new, original and timely interdisciplinary series that seeks to be pivotal in nature and improve our understanding of the role of the maritime sector within port economics and global supply chain management, shipping finance, and maritime business and economic history. The maritime industry plays an increasingly important role in the changing world economy, and this new series offers an outlet for reviewing trends and developments over time as well as analysing how such changes are affecting trade, transport, the environment and financial markets. Each title in the series will communicate key research findings, shaping new approaches to maritime economics. The core audience will be academic, as well as policymakers, regulators and international maritime authorities and organisations. Individual titles will often be theoretically informed but will always be firmly evidence-based, seeking to link theory to policy outcomes and changing practices.

More information about this series at
http://www.palgrave.com/gp/series/15187

Elvira Haezendonck · Alain Verbeke
Editors

Sustainable Port Clusters and Economic Development

Building Competitiveness through Clustering of Spatially Dispersed Supply Chains

palgrave
macmillan

Editors
Elvira Haezendonck
Department of Business
Vrije Universiteit Brussel (VUB)
Brussels, Belgium

Alain Verbeke
Haskayne School of Business
University of Calgary
Calgary, AB, Canada

Department of Business
Vrije Universiteit Brussel
Brussels, Belgium

Henley Business School
University of Reading
Reading, UK

Palgrave Studies in Maritime Economics
ISBN 978-3-030-40323-2 ISBN 978-3-319-96658-8 (eBook)
https://doi.org/10.1007/978-3-319-96658-8

Library of Congress Control Number: 2018951047

Cover credit: Hans Berggren/GettyImages/Fatima Jamadar

This Palgrave Macmillan imprint is published by the registered company Springer Nature Switzerland AG
The registered company address is: Gewerbestrasse 11, 6330 Cham, Switzerland

Dedicated to our beloved families

Foreword

Nearly every segment of international supply chains is seeking to rationalize its operations through mergers or strategic alliances. This includes shipping lines, terminal operators, and shippers. It would appear, when engaging in a superficial analysis, that port authorities remain the one notable exception to far-reaching cooperative arrangements, at least in relative terms, vis-à-vis other economic actors in the supply chain.

It is correct that cooperation between port authorities has not yet resulted in a major consolidation wave, in contrast to what has occurred in other segments of the chain. However, recent cases of consolidation at the port authority level do exist. One example is the well-reported case of Ghent and Zeeland Seaports, which merged into the "North Seaport" last year. Other recent mergers include those of Hamina and Kotka in Finland, and the state-owned port companies of Ningbo and Zhoushan in China. The Northwest Seaport Alliance is not a merger, but a far-reaching cooperation agreement between the ports of Seattle and Tacoma in the USA that joined the marine cargo operations of both ports. The North Seaport and the Northwest Seaport Alliance are examples of bottom-up cooperation. In contrast, the recent reform of the Italian port system, which reduced the number of port authorities from 25 to 14, is a top-down case. As the port authorities are owned by the central government, it was the Italian state that pushed forward this consolidation.

More consolidation of port authorities will become inevitable, given the developments in the market toward gaining scale and scope economies, but also given environmental and societal pressures. Land is a scarce good, and competition for land use is therefore very high. What complicates far-reaching forms of cooperation between port authorities are public ownership and related institutional impediments to common initiatives. An important precondition for successful cooperation projects therefore lies in the autonomy of port authorities. Port authorities should be free to determine the business case for cooperation and to act upon this. If such business case is missing, then the likelihood of success becomes a lot smaller.

In addition to formal mergers and alliances, there are many other ways in which port authorities cooperate today with a variety of stakeholders. Such cooperation can range from joint investments in hinterland connections to clean air programs. The ports in San Pedro Bay are a good example of the latter. We can expect a growing number of these initiatives, for instance, in the field of the "circular economy," whereby port authorities work together with their industrial clusters, inter alia, to give new economic purpose to waste products such as wastewater that was used to cool down industrial installations, and can be used further for urban heating purposes.

As a complement to regional collaboration, ports also cooperate in a "transoceanic" fashion. Think of initiatives such as ChainPort, a network started by the ports of Hamburg and Los Angeles, as a dissuasion tool against protective attitudes about data sharing. Or think of the World Ports Sustainability Program, a partnership between IAPH and several international port-related organizations to develop and showcase the global leadership of ports in contributing to the Sustainable Development Goals of the United Nations and to empower ports in providing sustainable value added to their communities.

The above suggests substantial levels of ongoing cooperation in the port sector, including joint initiatives at the level of port authorities. Mergers and alliances, however, do remain rather exceptional cases, and this is largely due to the institutional context within most port authorities function. Given the increasing number of port authorities becoming "corporatized" (meaning their morphing into business units with arm's length linkages with political decision makers)—and in some cases their privatization—it may be only a matter of time before we will witness more widespread consolidation, as observed in other segments of the supply chain.

I warmly welcome this exciting, new research volume by Elvira Haezendonck and Alain Verbeke, two leading scholars in the area of seaport strategic management. The different chapters in this book rigorously highlight the many drivers and impediments to seaport cooperation, both at the cluster level and beyond. This book will allow substantial reflection by enlightened seaport authorities and port cluster managers, on crafting win-win conditions for long-term, strategic collaboration.

One key lesson I have learned from reading this volume is that port authorities and port clusters alike should develop strategic capabilities in collaboration and understand the underlying industrial logic behind any cooperative initiative. Opportunistic "get-togethers," supported by some surface-scratching accounting data, are a particularly poor basis for long-term, strategic alliance formation involving seaports.

Antwerp, Belgium

Dr. Patrick Verhoeven
Managing Director—International Association of Ports and Harbors (IAPH)

Praise for *Sustainable Port Clusters and Economic Development*

"In an era of growing concerns about port clusters' externalities and their shift towards more international strategic cooperation and M&A activity, this book provides sound managerial advice on long-term, sustainable cluster development."

—Dr. Jan Hoffmann, *Chief, Trade Logistics Branch, Division on Technology and Logistics, UNCTAD and President of the International Association of Maritime Economists*

"As Series Editor, I am proud to include this 'jewel' in the collection: It delivers a fascinating and absorbing account on the role of cooperative initiatives in modern port management."

—Professor Hercules Haralambides, *Editor-in-Chief of Maritime Economics and Logistics, Texas A&M University, USA*

Contents

Contributors

Paul Brugman KBC Bank and Insurance, Brussels, Belgium

Michael Dooms Department of Business, Vrije Universiteit Brussel (VUB), Brussels, Belgium

Elvira Haezendonck Department of Business, Vrije Universiteit Brussel (VUB), Brussels, Belgium

Tim Jans Vrije Universiteit Brussel (VUB), Brussels, Belgium

Mychal Langenus Department of Business, Vrije Universiteit Brussel (VUB), Brussels, Belgium

Alain Verbeke Haskayne School of Business, University of Calgary, Calgary, AB, Canada; Department of Business, Vrije Universiteit Brussel, Brussels, Belgium; Henley Business School, University of Reading, Reading, UK

List of Figures

List of Tables

1

Introduction: Co-orchestrating Sustainable Port Ecosystems

Elvira Haezendonck and Alain Verbeke

1 Introduction

During the past few decades, a sharp increase has taken place in the number and scope of collaborative agreements involving seaports and a variety of actors in these ports' vertical and horizontal value chains. These collaborative agreements have been the subject of a large number of studies in the scholarly literature. Far-reaching port integration is hardly a new phenomenon, as illustrated by the well-known Copenhagen-Malmö

E. Haezendonck (✉)
Department of Business, Vrije Universiteit Brussel (VUB),
Brussels, Belgium
e-mail: elvira.haezendonck@vub.be

A. Verbeke
Haskayne School of Business, University of Calgary, Calgary, AB, Canada
e-mail: alain.verbeke@haskayne.ucalgary.ca

Department of Business, Vrije Universiteit Brussel, Brussels, Belgium

Henley Business School, University of Reading, Reading, UK

E. Haezendonck and A. Verbeke (eds.), *Sustainable Port Clusters and Economic Development*, Palgrave Studies in Maritime Economics,
https://doi.org/10.1007/978-3-319-96658-8_1

cross-border alliance, which dates back to 2001. However, it has been especially in the post-2008 period (starting with the "great recession") that worldwide managerial and scholarly attention has been devoted to deeper and broader collaborative arrangements involving seaports.

New forms of collaboration, including "coopetition," meaning the joint occurrence of cooperation and competition, have become common among seaports and among internationally distributed value chains. Such coopetition has become associated with sophisticated, new governance approaches to achieve efficient seaport functioning, often in spite of local, political resistance. The main features of these new governance forms are twofold. *First*, they include accounting for a broader range of benefits and costs associated with seaport activities, which have often become linked to a wider set of stakeholders. *Second*, these governance forms also recognize the need to assess carefully the distribution of costs and benefits across geographically dispersed economic actors, as a precondition for long-term seaport viability, growth, and economic performance, in terms of value creation and capture.

The new collaborative efforts thereby need to build on sound economic efficiency principles, with a focus on reducing costs, gaining scale and scope economies, and creating value-added across international logistics chains. New equilibria are being created, mostly with decentralized market power among, inter alia port authorities, cargo handling companies, industrial enterprises, exporters, distributors, shipping alliances, hinterland transport providers, and inland terminals. In line with Pitelis and Teece (2010), it could be argued—within the context of international value chains—that all of the above actors are involved in co-orchestrating port ecosystems. The uniqueness of these ecosystems is the collaboration between on the one hand; footloose multinational enterprises or firms located in foreign countries, and on the other hand; highly localized companies, embedded in clusters, with the port authorities often acting as linchpins or even "lead institutions" at the heart of these ecosystems. Important in this respect is the focus on joint opportunity generation and value creation throughout localized clusters and the international ecosystem. These ecosystems should therefore not be viewed as attempts to achieve collusion or market power, but rather as efficient governance systems with economizing properties, and sometimes with unexpected (but typically beneficial) spillover effects. For example, deep knowledge about partners embedded in a cluster may lead to a reciprocal reputation for reliability, cascading up or down the value chain, to affect other linkages among the partners involved (e.g., in the sphere of a common corporate social responsibility strategy).

2 Port Authorities as Co-orchestrators of Ecosystems

In order to create and capture value beyond the confines of a single company or beyond narrowly defined, geographic cluster borders, ports need entrepreneurial management capabilities that can actually foster ecosystem co-creation, in line with Pitelis and Teece (2010), Iansiti and Levien (2004), and Van der Lugt and De Langen (2018). Such management capabilities allow securing the longer-term viability, growth, and economic performance, in terms of value creation and capture, of individual firms, localized clusters, and international value chains.

Building upon modern resource-based view thinking, applied to the port context (see, i.e., Haezendonck et al. 2001; Gordon et al. 2005), this book explores the underlying motivations and decision-making processes adopted by port managers, to design and establish ecosystems that may reach far beyond the conventional geographic borders of seaports, with a view to create and capture value for the long term, and taking into account the goals and aspirations of a wide array of partners and other stakeholders.

We observed that some port authorities have selected a "portfolio approach," combining various forms of long-term strategic collaboration, whereas other ones have opted for a "staged" approach, with increasing levels of resource commitments over time. A first stage might involve the signing of a Memorandum of Understanding (MoU), whereas the final stage might be associated with a full-fledged merger or acquisition of another economic actor in the value chain. Early collaboration efforts are typically associated with high uncertainty and steep learning curves. Over time, a stronger familiarity ensues with the other actors in the ecosystem, and the related social capital creation with ecosystem partners can then reasonably lead to higher resource commitments, albeit often (necessarily) associated with reciprocal commitments so as to avoid the "dark side" of unilateral commitments (i.e., opportunistic behavior).

The organic processes described above, with escalating levels of reciprocal resource commitments, and virtuous cycles of social capital creation, often require not only formalized "contracting," but also relationship-building mechanisms in governance design. Especially when they focus on relational elements in ecosystem creation, port managers become the de facto co-orchestrators of global logistics chains, often operating in concert with a variety of other co-orchestrators such as global shipping companies. Here, much in line with Kano's (2017) analysis of value chain mapping, it is important to search for resource complementarities among ecosystem partners, so as to craft viable win-win governance approaches. If successful, ports de facto morph from system-integrators at the local or regional level, into co-orchestrators of ecosystems that are geographically much more widely dispersed.

3 Building Competitiveness Through Spatially Dispersed Value Chains and Localized Clusters

Many port (authority) managers are presently engaged in collaborative agreements with partners located in both their proximate geographic area and far beyond this area. The economic drivers of such cooperation can vary widely and include goals as diverse as an expected, stronger competitive position to attract and retain traffic flows, better access to capital, or an improved, overall control over the logistics chain. From a governance perspective, the cooperative agreements can range from top-down, government-influenced alliance formation to bottom-up, collaborative projects, and from long-term market contracting to full-fledged mergers. Much has been suggested, but little is actually known and researched about the performance outcomes of these cooperative efforts, especially in terms of overall, governance efficiency features and the related competitiveness of the economic actors and value chains or clusters involved. This book seeks to fill this dual knowledge gap.

In Chapter 2, we develop a new governance perspective on port–hinterland linkages and related port impacts. Many stakeholders in a port's hinterland now demand tangible economic benefits from port activities, as a precondition for supporting port expansion and infrastructural investments. We use a governance lens to assess this farsighted contracting challenge. We find that most contemporary economic impact assessments of port investment projects pay scant attention to the contractual relationship challenges in port-hinterland relationships. In contrast, we focus explicitly on the spatial distribution of such impacts and the related contractual relationship issues facing port authorities or port users and their stakeholders in the port hinterland. We introduce a new concept, the Port Hinterland Impact (PHI) matrix, which focuses explicitly on the spatial distribution of port impacts and related contractual relationship challenges. The PHI matrix offers insight into port impacts using two dimensions: logistics dedication, as an expression of Williamsonian asset specificity in the sphere of logistics contractual relationships, and geographic reach, with a longer reach typically reflecting the need for more complex contacting to overcome "distance" challenges with external stakeholders. We use the PHI matrix in our empirical, governance-based analysis of contractual relationships between the port authorities in Antwerp and Zeebrugge, and their respective stakeholders.

In Chapter 3, we focus on cross-border ecosystem co-creation. Despite the well-documented rise of international trade expansion, and related growth in foreign direct investment (FDI), little research has addressed explicitly the implications of these developments for cross-border exchanges and cooperation between firms in adjacent regions that belong to different countries. This lack of attention is surprising, given the typically low psychic distance features associated with such cooperation and the relative ease with which the "liability of outsidership" can be overcome, as compared to collaborative arrangements among economic actors located in regions that are located geographically further apart from each other. This chapter addresses the above issue of "liability of closeness," by analysing the perceptions of 101 firms from two adjacent regions in the European Union. We deploy an extended version of "Porter's diamond" model and find that despite many similarities between the two adjacent regions, a number of critical differences, typically neglected in work using mainstream distance indices, act a strong obstacles for unlocking—and capitalizing upon—economic opportunities awaiting in the adjacent region.

In Chapter 4, we highlight perceptions of disappointing competitive-advantage outcomes, associated with port collaboration that extends into the hinterland, thereby describing the challenges of ecosystem orchestration. Such orchestration may be of critical strategic importance to seaports, in an environmental context of increased scale of maritime operations and vessel sizes, stakeholder opposition to port expansion, and increasingly complex regulation. However, not every port is home to economic actors willing and capable of engaging in ecosystem co-orchestration and using such orchestration to gain competitive advantage. Adopting an extended resource-based view perspective, we analyzed the competitive strengths of the Antwerp port cluster, including the hinterland network linkages, building upon a large number of interviews with port experts. Against our expectations, which were based on insight from the mainstream literature on the efficiency advantages of collaboration, our analysis suggests that extensive linkages with the hinterland did not result in improved competitive advantage. One should therefore not assume automatically that paying more attention to port ecosystem building, will necessarily lead to positive economic outcomes.

In Chapter 5, we examine what role cluster organizations play in facilitating co-orchestration for ecosystem development. Based on an extension of the natural resource-based view of the firm, we assess whether and how geographically localized clusters can contribute to the proactivity of individual firms' environmental strategies. Clusters can develop a formal, shared resource-base through establishing actual "cluster organizations," and they can utilize these organizations to generate cluster-specific advantages. We perform a case study of the petrochemical cluster in the Antwerp port, building upon a review of relevant documents, complemented with in-depth interviews. We describe the relevant cluster organizations and their role. Furthermore, we describe a number of completed, joint projects with a tangible environmental impact. We look at the cluster's life cycle to understand why this particular cluster became so important for the firms in the cluster, in the realm of environmental issues. We conclude that this cluster has a number of idiosyncratic features that fostered longer-term collaboration than typically considered common for clusters, even during the later stages of its life cycle.

Chapter 6 describes how the cross-border Antwerp-Rotterdam Area petrochemical cluster (also called ARA cluster) has succeeded in co-creating ecosystem elements serving sustainability. A considerable number of research contributions have analyzed the net benefits for individual firms of either being embedded in a geographical cluster or deploying a proactive environmental strategy, but this study looks at the joint effects of cluster collaboration and proactive environmental strategy on competitive advantage for the firms involved. We provide insight into which positive effects were generated, and how, building upon Verbeke et al. (2006) extended natural resource-based theory of the firm. Our empirical work shows that the largest petrochemical cluster in Europe has positively influenced the firms embedded in it, to perform proactive environmental investments. Cluster-related parameters have increased the investments in the various resource domains identified in Hart's natural resource-based view model. In addition, the cluster has stimulated the development of eco-related capabilities, in particular higher-order learning and stakeholder integration. The enhanced capabilities derived from cluster membership have allowed the affected firms to improve their competitive position.

The five studies included in this volume compellingly demonstrate that seaports and seaport authorities can no longer operate as standalone entities, but must be sensitive to opportunities for collaborative action both inside the localized port cluster and beyond. Substantial economizing and value creating outcomes can result from efforts to co-orchestrate port-related ecosystems. In an era when competition increasingly revolves around both geographically localized clusters and internationally dispersed value chains, the careful mapping of which collaborative agreements can ultimately generate net economic benefits to the economic actors involved, is of critical importance. As is always the case with cooperative action, selectivity is required in determining which collaborative agreements will lead to the highest returns for port authorities and other actors interested in co-orchestrating port ecosystems.

References

Gordon, J. R., Lee, P. M., & Lucas, H. C., Jr. (2005). A resource-based view of competitive advantage at the Port of Singapore. *The Journal of Strategic Information Systems, 14*(1), 69–86.

Haezendonck, E., Pison, G., Rousseeuw, P., Struyf, A., & Verbeke, A. (2001). The core competences of the Antwerp seaport: An analysis of "port specific" advantages. *International Journal of Transport Economics/Rivista internazionale di economia dei trasporti, 28*(3), 325–349.

Iansiti, M., & Levien, R. (2004). *The keystone advantage: What the new dynamics of business ecosystems mean for strategy, innovation, and sustainability*. Boston, MA: Harvard Business School Press.

Kano, L. (2017). Global value chain governance: A relational perspective. *Journal of International Business Studies, 49*(6), 1–22.

Pitelis, C. N., & Teece, D. J. (2010). Cross-border market co-creation, dynamic capabilities and the entrepreneurial theory of the multinational enterprise. *Industrial and Corporate Change, 19*(4), 1247–1270.

Van der Lugt, L. M., & De Langen, P. W. (2018). Value creation and value capture in the ports' business system. In S. Pettit & A. Beresford (Eds.), *Port management* (pp. 13–27). London: Kogan Page.

Verbeke, A., Bowen, F., & Sellers, M. (2006, August). Corporate environmental strategy: Extending the natural resource-based view of the firm. In *Academy of Management Proceedings* (Vol. 2006, No. 1, pp. A1–A6). Briarcliff Manor, NY: Academy of Management.

2

A New Governance Perspective on Port–Hinterland Relationships: The Port Hinterland Impact (PHI) Matrix

Elvira Haezendonck, Michael Dooms and Alain Verbeke

1 Introduction

Notteboom and Rodrigue (2005) have convincingly argued that many ports have become more functionally integrated with their hinterlands, with ports acting as "impact hubs" for a broad region. The new economic geography of port impacts, which have become more spatially dispersed than in the past, is imposing new contractual relationship challenges on ports and on the various economic actors in their hinterland with whom contractual relationships need to be crafted and fine-tuned. A contractual relationship

E. Haezendonck (✉) · M. Dooms
Department of Business, Vrije Universiteit Brussel (VUB), Brussels, Belgium
e-mail: elvira.haezendonck@vub.be

A. Verbeke
Haskayne School of Business, University of Calgary, Calgary, AB, Canada
e-mail: alain.verbeke@haskayne.ucalgary.ca

Department of Business, Vrije Universiteit Brussel, Brussels, Belgium

Henley Business School, University of Reading, Reading, UK

E. Haezendonck and A. Verbeke (eds.), *Sustainable Port Clusters and Economic Development*, Palgrave Studies in Maritime Economics,
https://doi.org/10.1007/978-3-319-96658-8_2

refers to any economic exchange between two or more parties whereby these parties face the challenge of jointly selecting the most efficient "governance structure" for this exchange, given the characteristics of the transaction at hand. The presence of relationship-specific investments associated with an exchange, that is, dedicated investments that cannot be easily redeployed elsewhere without loss of economic value, calls for more complex contractual relations, and the extreme case being that of internalization (e.g., the vertical integration of activities in a supply chain), see Williamson (1979). Examples of new contractual relationships and challenges for ports can be found in van der Lugt et al. (2013) on the importance of inter-firm alliances in the port of Rotterdam and in Verhoeven (2010) on the role of port authorities as entrepreneurs and community managers.

Most large seaports in the Hamburg-Le Havre range have been able to manage the contracting pressures arising from stakeholders interested in a variety of "societal" economic impacts (as opposed to firm-level impacts) in the port area itself. Such societal impacts include, inter alia, effects related to employment (e.g., in the realm of worker compensation, contracting status, and health and safety issues) as well as environmental externalities. Achieving stakeholder consensus has occurred through extensive, dedicated managerial attention and investments from port authorities and port users, devoted to solving the above challenges. In return, port authorities and large-port users have often been able to safeguard or even recapture their "social license to operate." This license had become challenged for two reasons: first, many port activities being less visible to large parts of the communities located close to the port and experiencing negative port activity impacts; and second, activist community and environmental groups focusing on (alleged) negative social and environmental externalities of port activities. For example, many port authorities now use "green portfolio" approaches to guide modal shifts in hinterland transportation, thereby gaining renewed support from local stakeholders interested in mitigating environmental and health impacts (Haezendonck et al. 2009).

As a result of many port authorities' successful strategies in addressing intra-port stakeholder concerns, much of the debate on seaport expansion has shifted toward the wider, spatially distributed, effects of port development whereby "contracts" must be struck with a variety of stakeholders located in this broader geographic space. Here, economic impact assessments are often used as a methodology to support resource allocation and funding of new infrastructure projects for port development. Unfortunately, in most economic impact assessment reports, the spatial configuration and significance of economic impacts, and especially their distribution across stakeholders located outside of the port area, have only been given scant attention.

Economic impact assessments typically focus on aggregate effects, for example, in terms of employment and value added, based on aggregations of local port firms' impacts, and less focused on economic relations with actors located outside the port area, in particular for cargo ports (Dooms et al. 2010). However, stakeholders such as inland ports and terminals, logistics services providers, commercial and residential real estate developers, community groups, and various government agencies outside of the port area are often mainly interested in how port cargo ultimately affects activities unfolding in the particular geographic area where they operate or that falls under their jurisdiction, for example, in terms of value added created. Access to accurate information on spatially distributed economic impacts is a precondition for these economic actors to engage in farsighted contracting (in the spirit of Williamson 1996), with port authorities, for example, in terms of support for transport infrastructure expansion.

From a governance perspective, "new-generation" regional economic impact studies can therefore contribute to mitigating two main contracting challenges, namely bounded rationality (BRat) and bounded reliability (BRel) problems faced by the stakeholders involved (Verbeke and Greidanus 2009; Verbeke 2013). BRat problems reflect the scarcity of mind of the various stakeholders in terms of their ability to access, understand, and act upon accurate information on spatially distributed, port economic impacts. Regional economic impact studies, especially if consistent with the port authority's broader strategic planning efforts, can also reduce BRel challenges, or problems of scarcity of effort to make good on open-ended promises, experienced by the stakeholders involved. For example, open-ended promises made by the port authority, such as a long-term commitment to engage in dedicated investments toward ameliorating a particular logistics connection, become more credible when accurate information on the size and scope of cargo flows, as well as their economic value and the distribution thereof across time, space, and economic actors involved, is shared with the hinterland stakeholders.

In this chapter, we therefore introduce a new concept, the Port Hinterland Impact (PHI) matrix, which provides detailed insights into the hinterland impact of a port using two dimensions: logistics dedicatedness and geographic reach. We suggest that this matrix should be integrated into all future, port regional economic impact studies, because the information embedded in the matrix will support decision making and especially farsighted contracting between port authorities and economic actors in the hinterland, for example, with respect to the joint planning, funding, and usage of new, dedicated infrastructure.

The chapter is structured as follows: Sect. 2 discusses the importance of the extended hinterland when designing port economic impact assessments. Section 3 introduces the new concept of the PHI matrix. Section 4 includes a critical discussion of a number of PHI matrix applications and proposes a new research agenda. Section 5 concludes.

2 From Local to Regional Impacts: The Need for a Governance-Based Model

Since the rise of the container in the late 1960s, and especially during periods of economic recession, port stakeholders have become increasingly concerned about the decreasing employment and value added generated locally by ports in urban areas. Hall and Jacobs (2012, p. 189) even argued that the new logistics requirements of global trade routes and supply chain systems have made the joint, harmonious development of ports and the cities where they are located a vestige of the past. Here, port authorities, port users, and other stakeholders may need to establish new governance mechanisms[1]: (i) to guide the development and utilization of new transport infrastructure capacity; (ii) to encourage innovation; (iii) to address externalities; and (iv) to create, capture, and distribute economic value. The challenges at hand have been well described in the "dry port" and extended gateway literature (VIL 2006; Charlier 2011) whereby economic activities conventionally located inside the port are increasingly being "transferred" from the seaport to a "dry port," see, for example, McCalla (1999) and Roso et al. (2009).

Veenstra et al. (2012), but also Haralambides and Gujar (2011) and Iannone (2012), have argued that a better performance of the overall supply chain can often be achieved by extending the sea-terminal connection into the hinterland, thereby potentially generating increased overall benefits in terms of the logistics chain's performance, modal shift opportunities, and regional development effects. Here, the focus can be on developing environment-friendly logistics linkages between the port and its hinterland. In addition, appropriate infrastructure expansion and related services development strategies in the hinterland may allow the broader port region to create value added and employment, based upon maritime cargo, especially containers, through distribution centers performing value-added logistics (VAL) with a regional, national, and even continental reach. In Europe, this last category of centers is referred to as "European distribution centers" (EDCs) whereby typically substantial attention is devoted to mitigating environmental impacts.

Despite the fact that developments in port networks and extended gates are mainly driven by port authority and port user expansion strategies, as described by Roso and Lumsden (2010) and Roso et al. (2009), this "delegation" of activities toward the hinterland is likely also to involve the transfer of value added toward this same hinterland. Here, the concept of "delegation" may be somewhat inappropriate as various economic actors are involved in complex contracting, associated with the broader spatial distribution of economic activities.

For example, van der Horst and van der Lugt (2011) and Cullinane et al. (2012) interpreted the shift of VAL away from seaports into the hinterland as an expression of emergent, strategic freight networks, including a better spread of flows and terminals linked to or (partly) owned by the port, which guarantees critical volume and more fluid flows. Here, port networks entail much more, from a contracting perspective, than a single connection between a dry port and a seaport. However, Veenstra et al. (2012) have suggested that many network challenges have remained unexplored, such as potential trade-offs between port interests, terminal owner interests, and other network actors' interests.

A number of recent scholarly papers, such as van der Horst and van der Lugt (2011), Cullinane et al. (2012), and Veenstra et al. (2012), have focused on the benefits of dry ports for regional economic development. However, the potential trade-offs in terms of the creation of value added within the network, which give rise to complex contracting challenges, have been largely ignored. In this context, Hall and Jacobs (2012) have expressed their concern that the conventional port–city relationship will become increasingly complex, reflecting only a fraction of the contracting needed with multiple parties to establish viable logistics chains encompassing the hinterland. Here, it is critical to investigate not only the benefits, but also the costs and risks related to the dry port concept for the various stakeholders involved. The migration of port activities to the hinterland typically triggers specific governance and related contracting demands from these stakeholders.

Verbeke and Dooms (2008) and Wang and Ducruet (2012) have suggested that it may be difficult to quantify economic impacts from the perspective of all relevant stakeholders or for a well-defined geographic area affected by a port development project. In a 2008 paper, Verbeke and Dooms developed an integrative framework, covering relevant stakeholders and the wider geographical area, and an operational calculation model for long-term strategic port planning, based on origin–destination statistics of containers to VAL clusters in the hinterland. This model allows evaluating long-term port expansion trajectories, including impacts of new investment projects on the four main elements in the seaport system: the maritime transport component, the port activity component, the hinterland transport component, and the broader port network component. As one example of the relevance of this approach when applied to the port of Antwerp, Verbeke and Dooms (2008) found that the predicted, additional direct economic impacts of container projects in the Belgian port network component in terms of value creation and direct employment confirmed a shift from direct added value and direct employment creation within the port area to the wider region outside the port area.

However, large impacts on the broader port network were viewed as conditional upon the relevant public agencies, making available appropriate transport infrastructure and land for locating VAL activities in this network. Table 1 shows the results of the predicted impacts, associated with developing the port of Antwerp's extended gateway. Verbeke and Dooms' (2008) results were consistent with Notteboom and Rodrigue's (2005) earlier work, which documented the growth of the port of Antwerp's "extended gateway," thereby confirming the rise of port regionalization.

Robinson (2002) has argued that ports are mere elements in complex, logistics-driven value chains and are thereby involved in the

Table 1 Visualization of the analytical results

Additional impacts in the extended gateway	High growth		Low growth	
	Horizon 2015	Horizon 2030	Horizon 2015	Horizon 2030
Intermodal capacity demand (in TEU)[a]	884,346	1806.816	732,771	1,381,538
Intermodal capacity demand (in net meters)	2954	5902	1979	3869
Intermodal capacity demand (in net hectares)	33.7	78.3	23.7	54.0
Employment impact intermodal terminals (FTEs)	/	517	/	395
'Added value' impacts' intermodal terminals (million euros)	12.7	25.9	10.5	19.8
Land requirements for VAL—EDC	833	1.218	504	676
Employment impact VAL—EDC (FTEs)	44,763	65,448	27,103	36,328
Added Value impact VAL—EDC (million euros)	4102	5997	2482	3329

Notes TEU: twenty-foot equivalent unit; FTE: full-time equivalent; VAL: value-added logistics; EDC: European Distribution Center

[a]Including the demand from the port of Rotterdam affecting the Belgian intermodal barge network (approx. 1/3 of total demand)

Source Verbeke and Dooms (2008)

processes of value creation, capture, and distribution. Therefore, from a governance perspective, the main challenge for the stakeholders involved is to generate and utilize effectively information on spatially distributed economic impacts. In concrete terms, this comes down to economizing on BRat and BRel, two concepts defined above and reflecting, respectively, "scarcity of mind" and "scarcity of effort to make good on open-ended promises." For example, economizing on BRat and BRel can be achieved by showing unambiguously to all stakeholders, which part of overall economic value is (or will be) generated by whom, in which part of the chain and in which locations. Unfortunately, as already noted above, most prior studies including Bryan et al. (2006) consider only local port impacts, including assessments of the impacts on suppliers to the maritime and industrial cluster (by estimating multipliers), as well as spending impacts in the local economy by the port workers.

In addition to analyzing expected economic impacts from the perspective of different stakeholders, the analysis should be done for different types of cargo as well and not only focus on containerized goods, which has mostly been the case in recent studies on dry ports. In addition, any analytical model adopted should be generally applicable to port networks and not be dependent on the availability of aggregated data, devoid of a spatial component.

Here, we must point out that completing Table 1 (in the realm of container traffic) requires the availability of transparent and reliable data on the origin/destination of containers, the spatial productivity of inland containers terminals, the spatial productivity of logistics activities in the port network, employment per hectare, added value per hectare, and capacity utilization of the actual intermodal terminals and logistics activities (e.g., warehouses). In the Belgian case, and for container traffic, these data were readily available from several prior studies.

Unfortunately, for other traffic categories (such as new cars, conventional cargo), a large number of these parameters were not available. Therefore, the use of this methodology (we refer to Dooms and Verbeke [2006] for a detailed insight into the method used) is presently limited to large container ports whereby data on these ports' hinterland and logistics network are readily available. From a governance perspective, however, we should emphasize that this type of information is critical to successful, complex contracting with economic actors in the port's hinterland and broader network.

We also observed two further complexities, based on various consulting studies (mainly port economic impact assessments) and academic papers (Gripaios and Gripaios 1995; De Brucker et al. 1998; Bryan et al. 2006; Haezendonck 2007). First, stakeholder opposition against port development projects has strongly increased in the last few decades, driven, inter alia, by a stakeholder focus on ecological and mobility impacts. But even beyond these impacts, some entrenched stakeholders also tend to resist increased competition and efficiency, as well as modern labor regulations in line with technological and organizational advances (e.g., the opposition to widely suggested changes of the "Major" law regulating port labor in Belgium) and so on. Stakeholders opposing further port expansion have sometimes credibly argued that the data included in port economic impact assessments had been artificially inflated, thus providing further ammunition against the case for new port development. Port authorities and port users engaged in promoting exaggerated economic impact estimations have thereby lost substantial credibility with many stakeholders, whose initial commitment to port development, or at least the acceptance thereof, has declined as a result. These actors increasingly view port authorities and port users as intrinsically unreliable contracting partners, who will not hesitate to embellish data when it suits their public relations' goals vis-à-vis their network partners. The relevant port authorities' and port users' unreliability appears to have backfired and has negatively affected contracting relationships with network partners.

Second, a number of port impact benchmarking studies have been conducted, but these typically do not conform to minimum standards of transparency in terms of concepts used, methodologies adopted, and comparative analyses performed. Imperfect data and imperfect comparisons among such studies amount to a serious BRat problem. Ill-conceived benchmarking triggers further disagreements among economic actors with a stake in port development on the actual impacts of port-related activities and the geographic distribution thereof. Such benchmarking studies, instead of providing useful information to guide managerial improvements toward best practices, trigger conflict among stakeholders as to the veracity of particular sets of information, thereby potentially resulting in delayed or contested resources. BRat problems are exacerbated rather than mitigated and accusations of unreliability abound.

Whence, the development of an accurate, generally applicable model to measure PHIs in economic terms, including a standardized methodology, is advisable in order to alleviate BRat and BRel problems. An appropriate model should take into account where economic value is actually generated in the hinterland and be sufficiently accurate for all stakeholders at different geographical levels to rely on the results for (future) investment decisions and related contracting with other stakeholders. A model conducive to economizing by reducing BRat and BRel challenges is likely to contribute to wider stakeholder support and acceptance of port activity and expansion projects.

3 Spatially Distributed Impacts of Port Activity: Introduction of the Port Hinterland Matrix Concept

A port's spatially distributed impacts refer to the direct and indirect effects beyond those arising inside the port area. Here, two parameters must be included in any analysis focused on governance and contracting challenges in the port economic system.

The first parameter represents a quantitative element, namely the port's geographic reach, starting from the left of Fig. 1: How much of the port traffic coming into—or moving out of—the port—travels, for example, 100 or more kilometers from and into the hinterland? Of the remaining traffic, how much travels 50 km or more? Or between 25 and 50 km? This parameter is important as it defines the economic actors with a stake in port development beyond the port area itself. A longer reach typically reflects transactions with higher logistics and regulatory complexity. More distance may also involve an increasing port market contest-ability, which could then lead to changing or wider port ranges

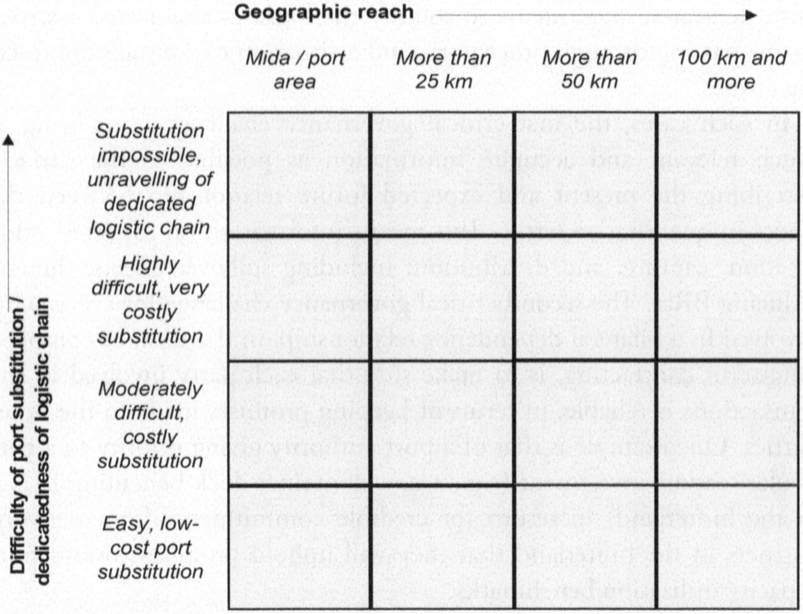

Fig. 1 PHI matrix (geographic reach and dedicatedness). MIDA: Maritime industrial development area

of competing ports. An analysis should be conducted of the port's reach for each traffic category since the actors involved in each "strategic traffic unit" (e.g., containers, general cargo, liquid bulk, and dry bulk) are likely very different.

The second parameter in Fig. 1 is a qualitative element, reflecting asset specificity: How difficult is port substitution or how dedicated is the logistics chain involved? The answer ranges from having minimal, low-cost substitution difficulties to the case of quasi-destruction of the value chain, if the port infrastructure were removed or became inaccessible. Importantly, a dedicated logistics chain, where economic actors are closely tied to one port with no—or very expensive—alternatives available, creates a situation of bilateral dependency. Such bilateral dependency is not restricted to relationships occurring inside the port area, but may involve, inter alia, the port authority or local port users and stakeholders outside of the port area. Here, both sets of actors can benefit from dedicated investments to solidify the logistics chain vis-à-vis rival chains passing through other ports and a situation of complex contracting ensues.

In such cases, the first critical governance challenge is to bring as much relevant and accurate information as possible to the surface, describing the present and expected future relationship between the actors in quantitative terms. This means information on expected value creation, capture, and distribution, including spillover effects, thereby reducing BRat. The second critical governance challenge for every actor involved in a bilateral dependency relationship, in the form of complex, long-term contracting, is to make sure that each party involved in the transactions is reliable, in terms of keeping promises made to the other parties. One example is that of a port authority giving priority to a particular seaport investment (e.g., a new container dock benefiting EDCs in the hinterland) in return for credible commitments from network partners in the hinterland that they will uphold promises toward port capacity utilization benchmarks.

Building upon the above analysis, a port's position in Fig. 1 can be linked to the value of the cargo, transported efficiently thanks to the logistics chain going through the port. In the case of high logistics dedicatedness, there would be a loss inflicted on all economic actors involved in case the port did not exist or were not accessible. This reflects an opportunity cost: "What in case the port did not exist?" However, this opportunity cost cannot be simply measured through calculating transport cost differentials with alternative logistics chains. Whereas transport cost differentials are real and should be taken into account, the more important point, from a governance perspective, is that the economic actors involved have engaged in irreversible investments that cannot be redeployed elsewhere without a severe economic loss.

If both the port's geographic reach extends further and logistics chain dedicatedness is higher (meaning a higher opportunity cost if the port were not accessible), the spatial distribution effect is stronger, and the contracting challenges more severe. A strong regional effect can then be expressed in monetary terms by assessing the value of the goods going through the port. This is a regional flow that would be disrupted if the port could not be accessed. In other words, the economic contributions of ports are not limited to local value added and employment, but can also be proxied by the value of the goods that pass through these ports in the context of international trade relationships. These value-added figures should be properly assessed: Geographically dispersed economic systems often thrive to a large extent thanks to efficient logistics chains, with seaports at their heart, that connect localized port clusters with the broader economy.

In addition, this regional effect in terms of the estimated value of goods flowing through regionally distributed logistics chains is only the tangible expression of multiple, underlying contracting relationships involving a multitude of economic actors, and with the logistics dedicatedness being a proxy for this underlying complexity.

In the next section, we will briefly discuss two applications of the above framework. The first application was completed in the context of the IMPACTE (Intermodal Port Access & Commodities Transport in Europe) project whereby a PHI matrix was developed for 11 Channel Ports located in the UK, Belgium, and France. The second application is an application to the port of Antwerp (Belgium).

4 Application of the PHI Matrix

All data for the IMPACTE study were collected during an 18-month period, with the European Commission co-funding the project (through the European Reconstruction and Development Fund) and with 27 ports and regional authorities from Belgium, France, and the UK being involved. The second study was a 6-month research study commissioned by the Antwerp Port Authority to determine the economic significance of logistics activities in the port hinterland. We created large data sets with quantitative data on trade flows (origin–destination statistics and value data) and conducted in-depth interviews with several port authorities, port operators, shipping lines, as well as industrial companies (see below for a detailed description of our approach to compose PHI matrices in each case).

We used as the basis for our analysis for each port the traffic volumes passing through this port (2006 data were available for each port). The data sources included official maritime statistics (particularly for the UK ports), data published by port authorities on their Web sites (e.g., Ostend, Zeebrugge, and Calais), information obtained directly from the port authorities, and the researchers' in-depth market knowledge from prior studies.

Wherever possible, ingoing and outgoing traffic flow data were compiled per mode of appearance (e.g., dry bulk and containers). Each of these traffic flows has idiosyncratic characteristics in terms of likely distance of transport toward the hinterland, market share distribution among inland transport modes, and value of the freight. For example, dry bulk cargoes usually have a relatively low value and are likely to be distributed only within a short distance inland, whereas "accompanied" roll-on/roll-off (RoRo) traffic typically has a very high value and is likely to be transported over long distances. In contrast, lift-on/lift-off container traffic, though also distributed over long distances, is much more suitable for inland distribution by rail and inland navigation.

The analysis of each port's reach into the hinterland was based on a variety of sources. For example, in ports such as Dover and Calais for RoRo traffic, recent surveys had been carried out that provided the necessary inputs for our analysis. In other ports, data from the MDS Transmodal GB (Great Britain) Freight Model were used, supplemented by market knowledge from in-depth interviews with port users and port authorities.

The cargo flows were then allocated to the various "distance" categories in the PHI matrix (<25 km, 25–50 km, 50–100 km, and >100 km), in order to understand the port's hinterland reach for each specific cargo category. An average value per ton of freight by broad commodity type was calculated based on UK trade statistics for 2006 at a Standard International Trade Classification 2-digit level. Our analysis allowed an estimate of the value in Euro of the cargo passing through each port per mode of appearance. The generalized cost of inland distribution per ton of cargo for each mode of appearance was calculated using some simple cost models for each mode.

The logistics dedicatedness dimension was analyzed through in-depth interviews with port users, such as terminal operators' shipping companies and forwarders. For each port, and each traffic category, we surveyed a number of port users representing a significant market share in the port traffic portfolio. For each cargo component (as represented in the matrix shown in Fig. 2, namely liquid bulk, dry bulk, containers, conventional cargo, and RoRo) in terms of geographic reach, we asked experts to assess the degree of logistics dedicatedness.

The experts consulted included the port users mentioned above, as well as members of regional and national port organizations and committees. Based on this qualitative information, we assigned each traffic flow segment to a particular cell in the PHI matrix. Here, we used

Geographic reach →

Dependency on the port / dedicatedness of logistic chain ↑	*Mida / port area*	*More than 25 km*	*More than 50 km*	*100 km and more*
Very strong dependence on the port	DryB (100%) 84.0 mln € LiqB (37.0%) 545 mln €	LiqB (1.6%) 30 mln €	LiqB (12.3%) 231 mln €	LiqB (49.1%) 924 mln €
Strong dependence on the port	GenC (1.4%) 16 mln €	GenC (1.4%) 16 mln €	GenC (4.6%) 51 mln €	GenC (92.6%) 1,019 mln €
Moderate dependence on the port			Cont (2.0%) 1,950 mln €	
Low dependence on the port	RoRo (0.9%) 474 mln € Cont (1.0%) 975 mln €	RoRo (1.9%) 978 mln € Cont (2.0%) 1,950 mln €	RoRo (3.9%) 1,991 mln €	RoRo (93.3%) 47,651 mln € Cont (95%) 92,640 mln €

Fig. 2 PHI matrix for the port of Zeebrugge (based on 2006 data). *Notes* RoRo (93.3%) means that 93.3% of the RoRo traffic is situated in that section of the matrix; €47,651 million: this represents 93.3% of the total RoRo value (€51,095 million); data are colored in red if the value of the cargo exceeds €10 billion; "very strong" dependence implies that port substitution is not feasible and would trigger the unraveling of the dedicated logistics chain; "strong" dependence implies highly difficult, very costly, but technically feasible port substitution

origin–destination data for each cargo type and gathered information on the volume as well as the (total) value of these goods. We also identified the degree to which these flows are footloose, i.e., whether these flows could easily be moved to another port. After an initial matrix was produced, we validated the results at the port authority level.

The application of the PHI matrix to 11 Belgian, UK, and French ports in the Channel Straits suggests that many traffic categories in most ports in each of the three countries are rather footloose, that is, can relatively easily move from one port to another as a function of transportation cost optimization. At the micro-level, this conclusion may be somewhat disturbing, since each port authority and port company operator would prefer to have international logistics chains heavily dependent and committed to the port over long periods of time. In reality, simple market contracting rules. Here, footloose cargo flows are an expression of a well-functioning, competitive port system whereby efficiency considerations or lower transport costs drive the structuring of logistics chains and port choice. In this context, we should emphasize, however, that the footloose nature of many traffic categories only holds for relatively small traffic shifts in the short run, as capacity constraints in other ports would prevent large-scale moves of cargo from one port to another.

For purposes of illustration, we show the PHI matrix for the port of Zeebrugge. On the basis of Fig. 2, the regional impact of Zeebrugge is a mixed story. The logistics chains for container and RoRo cargo are rather footloose (as is the case with many ports for these cargo types), suggesting the dominance of short-term market contracting. However, this observation does not hold for other cargo flows such as Liquid Natural Gas, with some flows locally embedded in the port through large-scale, non-redeploy able investments by a gas distribution company, and other flows more widely distributed across geographic space. On the basis of the interviews with port users and logistics operators in the hinterland, there are some indications that the Zeebrugge port authority is attempting to develop stronger linkages with inland hubs and is seeking strategic partnerships with reciprocal investments from cargo recipients engaged in VAL in the hinterland (e.g., Zeebrugge's cooperation and rail connection with Dourges in the North of France and Zeebrugge's Port connect estuary shipping products on Antwerp and Rotterdam).

We also created a PHI matrix for the port of Antwerp, a very large and diversified port with annual cargo flows exceeding 190 million tons (data from 2008). We gathered and analyzed quantitative data on origin–destination relationships for various cargo flows, starting with 12 in-depth interviews with port users. Here, we focused on gaining insights into both the geographic reach and logistical dedicatedness of each cargo flow. Special attention was devoted to the container sector, which has been growing in relative importance over the past two decades.

Initially, we defined 12 cargo flows for positioning in the PHI matrix: fruit, forest products, steel and other metal products, other conventional cargo, iron ore, cars, other RoRo traffic, containers (with a split among containers transported by road, rail, and inland navigation), fertilizers, grain and cereals, crude oil, and other liquid bulk. After the interviews, we concluded that a number of proposed cargo flows needed to be decomposed further into subcategories, and a number of additional categories needed to be included in the analysis to obtain more meaningful results. We decomposed the container flows into merchant haulage (MH) and carrier haulage (CH) (see below); forest products into paper, wood, pulp, and kaolin; and dry bulk into grains, fertilizers, blue stone, zinc and lead concentrates, ores, and coal.

Importantly, based on the interviews conducted, we concluded that the unbundling of the port's geographic reach in segments covering 25, 50, 100, and 100+ km (as used in the IMPACTE research) was not an appropriate decomposition for the port of Antwerp in order to obtain meaningful results. The interviewees suggested geographic segments of 0–50 km, 50–100 km, 100–200 km, and 200 km and beyond. The interviewees also suggested to take into account a few additional cargo flows such as other dry bulk (malt, plastic grains), project cargo, and secondhand cars. They also proposed to decompose further forest products, containers, and dry bulk (see below).

As regards logistical dedicatedness, some interviewees thought that the port of Antwerp has historically neglected to implement a strategy to attract regional, European headquarters of shipping lines (in particular in the container sector), thereby missing an opportunity to achieve higher logistics dedicatedness to the port. They viewed the port of Rotterdam as a best practice. The respondents thought that future investments to attract regional headquarters would be instrumental in increasing the logistical dedicatedness of the traffic category involved.

In the realm of container traffic, a distinction should be made between MH and CH. CH containers typically have a longer geographic reach but are less dedicated or committed to a port. Large carriers can typically restructure their transport corridors and do not need to include a particular port for specific transport and logistics operations. With CH, a critical mass of cargo allows to switch in a cost-effective fashion to alternative modes and/or ports. However, CH-induced port shifts can involve substantial port capacity availability requirements, which may not always be present in competing ports in the short run.

MH cargo flows tend to be smaller and have a more restricted geographic reach. However, these flows are typically also more "dedicated" to a specific port or port operator, agent, or forwarder, with whom privileged, long-term contracting relationships are maintained. The reason is that the firms driving MH (e.g., large manufacturing firms) are typically embedded in specific locations themselves, sometimes close to a port, and want to invest in stable logistics chains with high-quality services, which guarantee the absence of supply interruptions.

Consistent with the situation of the Channel Ports, the interviewees identified the growing importance of extended gateways for containers whereby port authorities should engage in longer-term relational contracting with other key economic actors in the networks that drive the main container flows, an insight consistent with the work of Notteboom and Rodrigue (2005) and Verbeke and Dooms (2008). Such relational contracting implies a reduced focus on immediate, short-term transport cost minimization and greater emphasis on longer-term elements such as reliability in service quality and security of supply. In this context, the content of the containers can also play an important role in determining the desirability of establishing long-term relationships with specific economic actors. For example, some stuffed and stripped containers are dedicated to a port because of the required logistics expertise and productivity, which may not be available in other ports (e.g., the port of Antwerp's superiority in handling containers filled with unprocessed tobacco).

The interviewees observed a general decrease in cargo flows' dependency on the port of Antwerp, that is, a loss of logistics dedicatedness, which is the opposite of what most port authorities would like to see. The interviewees argued that many cargo flows can now easily shift, that is, would incur low redeployment costs when shifting from one port to another because most competitors have access to the same level of know-how and technology, for example, for grain, new vehicles, coal, and ores. However, in the short run, large-scale shifts usually remain rare because of capacity constraints in competing ports.

Figure 3 shows the PHI matrix for the port of Antwerp. For a correct interpretation of the PHI matrix, the following elements need to be taken into account. First, when no specific percentages are mentioned for a particular cargo flow, this implies that the entire cargo volume is positioned in a single cell of the matrix. Second, where percentages are mentioned, the sum of all percentages in the matrix for a particular cargo flow (e.g., forest products or containers) should equal 100%. Third, where relevant, the specific port user and/or the hinterland mode used and/or the country of origin/destination is mentioned for specific cargo flows.

The port of Antwerp has become weaker as far as logistical dedicatedness for project cargo with high value added is concerned. This is at least partially the result of the lack of specialized investments in the port to attract this cargo type, but also because of the higher costs in Antwerp where "self-handling" possibilities are lacking, in contrast to the prevailing logistics practices in competing ports.

For a series of cargo flows, the port has been able to maintain strong logistics dedicatedness, namely for fruit and other conventional cargo, liquid bulk, forest products, blue stone and kaolin, used cars, fertilizers, and the crude oil for Antwerp's industrial cluster. In each case, port users have engaged in substantial "cargo-flow-specific" investments that have boosted the port's attractiveness.

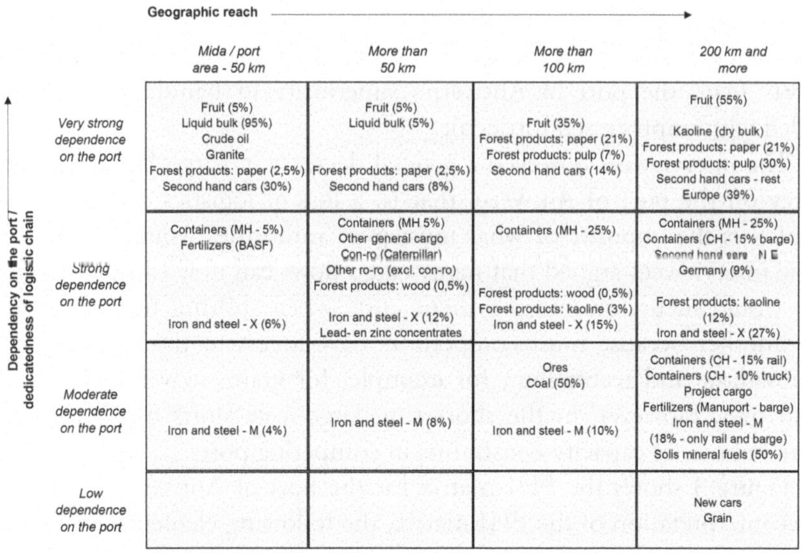

Fig. 3 Port Hinterland Impact matrix for the port of Antwerp (based on 2008 data). *Notes* MH: Merchant Haulage, CH: Carrier Haulage, X: Exports, M: Imports & BASF, Manuport, Caterpillar: specific port users

5 Limitations

In the two cases above, the PHI matrix provides insight into the regional impact of ports in terms of logistical dedicatedness and geographic reach of cargo flows. However, our analysis has a number of important limitations. First, the analyses included in this chapter were based on time-sensitive data. A more dynamic approach, showing cargo flow shifts in the PHI matrix, would undoubtedly enrich the analysis.

Second, for strongly diversified ports, more disaggregated data collection would be advisable for a correct interpretation of the results. However, it may become very costly to collect disaggregated origin–destination data and information on the value of goods on a regular basis and for the multiple cargo flows to be considered. If the PHI matrix is used to benchmark ports in a competitive setting, a port-range-based collection of data would be appropriate, which of course requires more resources and raises data availability and comparability problems.

Third, the port of Antwerp case suggests a linkage between the two axes of the PHI matrix. Strong logistics dedicatedness typically appears to be linked with a short geographic reach, whereas footloose traffic is usually associated with a longer geographic reach. From a hinterland/network perspective, this result is hardly unexpected since longer distances imply more overlap among port hinterlands and hence may result in fiercer port competition.

Fourth, the research team strongly depended on expert information to determine the level of logistics dedicatedness. Efforts should be made to measure directly port dependence or logistics dedicatedness through asset specificity-related variables, in order to obtain more robust results.

Fifth, the scale, function, competitive situation, and governance of a particular port may require a customized approach when attempting to operationalize the PHI matrix' dimensions, for example, in terms of relevant "distance segments" for the geographic reach variable and the specific proxies used to assess logistical dedicatedness, that is, the presence or absence of particular assets and investments with low redeploy-ability potential in other logistics chains.

Sixth, within the framework of the IMPACTE study discussed above, the PHI matrix was considered primarily a communications and public relations tool by some partner ports and regional authorities involved in the project. In contrast, in the port of Antwerp case, the operationalization of the PHI matrix morphed into an in-depth reflection on the proper governance of contractual relations with hinterland stakeholders. The question therefore arises how the PHI matrix is presently used as a strategic governance tool to support farsighted contracting with a variety of external stakeholders whereby important, dedicated logistics chains deserve substantial managerial attention to the micro-level detail of establishing efficient contractual relationships with external stakeholders. It would certainly be worthwhile to compare applications and to analyze whether achieving strategic governance goals, in terms of reducing BRat and BRel challenges and creating an organizational context for managing complex transactions in their entirety, has been facilitated by using this matrix.

6 Conclusion

We have developed a new governance perspective on the challenges facing port authorities and port users when contracting with the various economic actors in the port's hinterland. We have introduced the PHI matrix as a new analytical tool to support "optimal" contracting, whether explicit or implicit, with such hinterland actors. The PHI matrix, if used as a governance tool, allows reducing in a substantive fashion BRat and BRel problems in contracting. BRat problems are reduced by identifying and highlighting three types of data critical to contracting and broader strategic decision making by port authorities and hinterland actors, namely: (i) quantitative (volume-related) hinterland origin–destination statistics; (ii) information on the value of the traded cargo; and (iii) qualitative information on the logistics dedicatedness of traffic segments. The first two information sets provide an initial indication as to where senior managerial attention should be devoted to, in order to improve further logistics efficiency. If in addition to representing a large cargo volume and value, a particular traffic segment is also associated with substantial logistics dedicatedness, this should trigger more complex contracting schemes because of various types of specific assets involved (e.g., dedicated and interconnected infrastructure components in the logistics network).

BRel problems are mitigated because the PHI matrix eliminates information asymmetries between contracting parties: Both the absolute importance and relative importance of a particular hinterland actor for the port authority and port users are highlighted, and this sets the stage for "contractual negotiations" in terms of the joint development of new projects, the determination of the importance for the various actors of taking equity stakes in specific ventures, and so on. Obviously, each economic actor in the hinterland should be able to develop its own hinterland port impact (HPI) matrix as the mirror image of the PHI matrix at the port level. An HPI matrix is required to assess the port's importance to the stakeholder in quantitative and qualitative terms, both now and in the future. Such HPI matrix is critical especially in cases whereby dedicated joint investment projects with high asset specificity are contemplated.

Our new matrix represents a critical complement of traditional value-added and employment-related impact analyses, which are typically restricted to a narrow geographic zone and are devoid of insight into the nature of contractual relationships with actors located outside of the port and immediately adjacent geographic areas. Such analyses offer little insight into how relationships with spatially dispersed stakeholders in the port's broader geographic environment should be governed. It could be argued, mistakenly, that the PHI matrix also carries with it increased risks. For example, if it appears that a particular port traffic segment generates little value added locally (but high value added within the larger region) and has a rather footloose character, local stakeholders in the port area or adjacent to it might well withdraw their support from dedicated investments supporting these traffic segments. But the occurrence of such situation should be considered consistent with efficient governance: from a farsighted contracting perspective, highly asset-specific investments should be made by the actors who will benefit most from these investments and are willing to engage in complex contracting (with vertical integration being the most far-reaching contracting form in cases of very high asset specificity). Such investments should not be made by actors such as the port authority, or local port users, who are spatially embedded in the port, but would not be the primary beneficiaries of a particular traffic segment's growth and related logistics chain improvements.

The obvious caveat associated with low local stakeholder involvement in logistics chains, where these stakeholders experience little direct economic impacts of a particular traffic segment, is that spillovers must be taken into account. Individual traffic segments typically do not exist in a vacuum, but can contribute to both virtuous cycles of port expansion and vicious cycles of port contraction. For example, if local stakeholders withhold their support from investment projects with little immediate economic benefit accruing to them, but this affects negatively the port's overall competitive position, for example, vis-à-vis shipping companies operating in the port's foreland, such spillover should be factored into strategic decision making. Individual traffic segments in a port cannot necessarily be isolated from other segments in sophisticated logistics chains and certainly do not materialize in an institutional vacuum.

We welcome further intellectual dialogue on our new, governance-based approach to port–hinterland relationships. More debate among scholars and managers involved in strategic decision making on large-scale port investments will undoubtedly shed more light on both the potential, generalized relevance, and the limits of our PHI matrix. We are hopeful that the PHI matrix, as an analytical tool supporting economizing behavior by both port authorities and hinterland actors, will ultimately lead to improved, farsighted governance of port–hinterland relationships.

Acknowledgements Data for the Zeebrugge empirical case in this chapter were collected by the authors through the EU-supported IMPACTE study (Intermodal Ports Access and Commodities Transport in Europe—The Economic Role of Ports, 2008).

Note

1. A governance-based model, as referred to in the title of this section, has been successfully introduced in some major seaports in the Low Countries, such as Antwerp and Rotterdam, based on these ports' experience in consensus management, and shows that this type of model is in fact feasible in practice.

References

Bryan, J., Munday, M., Pickernell, D., & Roberts, A. (2006). Assessing the economic significance of port activity: Evidence from ABP operations in industrial South Wales. *Maritime Policy and Management, 33*(4), 371–386.

Charlier, J. (2011). Hinterlands, port regionalisation and extended gateways: The case of Belgium and Northern France. In P. Hall, R. McCalla, C. Comtois, & B. Slack (Eds.), *Integrating seaports and trade corridors*. Burlington-Farnham: Ashgate.

Cullinane, K., Bergqvist, R., & Wilmsmeier, G. (2012). The dry port concept—Theory and practice. *Maritime Economics & Logistics, 14*(1), 1–13.

De Brucker, K., Verbeke, A., & Winkelmans, W. (1998). *Sociaal-economische evaluatie van overheidsinvesteringen in transportinfrastructuur*. Leuven: Garant.

Dooms, M., & Verbeke, A. (2006). An integrative framework for long-term strategic seaport planning: An application to the port of Antwerp. In T. Notteboom (Ed.), *Ports are more than piers. Liber Amicorum presented to Prof. Dr. Willy Winkelmans* (pp. 173–192). Antwerp, Belgium: De Lloyd.

Dooms, M., Haezendonck, E., & Verbeke, A. (2010). *Towards a toolkit for port related socio-economic impacts: A meta-analysis of socio-economic impact studies conducted for seaports*. Edition: Econship 2011. Chios, Greece.

Gripaios, P., & Gripaios, R. (1995). The impact of a port on its local economy: The case of Plymouth. *Maritime Policy & Management, 22*(1), 13–24.

Haezendonck, E. (2007). *Transport project evaluation: Extending the cost-benefit approach*. Chaltenham: Edward Elgar Publishing.

Haezendonck, E., Dooms M., & Verbeke, A. (2009). *Green benchmarking: Green portfolio analysis as a strategic tool for competitive positioning*. Paper submitted for the 2009 Academy of Management Conference.

Hall, P. V., & Jacobs, W. (2012). Why are maritime ports (still) urban, and why should policy-makers care? *Maritime Policy & Management, 39*(2), 189–206.

Haralambides, H., & Gujar, G. (2011). The Indian dry ports sector, pricing policies and opportunities for public-private partnerships. *Research in Transportation Economics, 33*(1), 51–58.

Iannone, F. (2012). The private and social cost efficiency of port hinterland container distribution through a regional logistics system. *Transportation Research Part A: Policy and Practice, 46*(9), 1424–1448.

McCalla, R. J. (1999). Global change, local pain: Intermodal seaport terminals and their service areas. *Journal of Transport Geography, 7*(4), 247–254.

Notteboom, T., & Rodrigue, J. P. (2005). Port regionalization: Towards a new phase in port development. *Maritime Policy and Management, 32*(3), 297–313.

Robinson, R. (2002). Ports as elements in value-driven chain systems: The new paradigm. *Maritime Policy & Management, 29*(3), 241–255.

Roso, V., & Lumsden, K. (2010). A review of dry ports. *Maritime Economics & Logistics, 12*(2), 196–213.

Roso, V., Woxenius, J., & Lumsden, K. (2009). The dry port concept: Connecting container seaports with the hinterland. *Journal of Transport Geography, 17*(5), 338–345.

van der Horst, M. R., & van der Lugt, L. M. (2011). Coordination mechanisms in improving hinterland accessibility: Empirical analysis in the port of Rotterdam. *Maritime Policy & Management, 38*(4), 415–435.

van der Lugt, L., Dooms, M., & Parola, F. (2013). Strategy making by hybrid organisations: The case of the port authority. *Research in Transportation Business & Management, 8,* 103–113.

Veenstra, A., Zuidwijk, R., & van Asperen, E. (2012). The extended gate concept for container terminals: Expanding the notion of dry ports. *Maritime Economics & Logistics, 14*(1), 14–32.

Verbeke, A. (2013). *International business strategy: Rethinking the foundations of global corporate success*. Cambridge, UK: Cambridge University Press.

Verbeke, A., & Dooms, M. (2008). *Integrating the extended gateway concept in long-term strategic seaport planning: A European case study.* Conference Proceedings of the Van Horne Institute's 2007 Pacific Gateway Round Table. Canada: University of Calgary.

Verbeke, A., & Greidanus, N. (2009). The end of the opportunism versus trust debate: Bounded reliability as a new envelope concept in research on MNE governance. *Journal of International Business Studies, 40,* 1471–1495.

Verhoeven, P. (2010). A review of port authorirty functions: Towards a renaissance? *Maritime Policy and Management, 37*(4), 247–270.

VIL (Flanders Institute for Logistics). (2006). *Annual report 2005.* Antwerp: VIL.

Wang, C., & Ducruet, C. (2012). New port development and global city making: Emergence of the Shanghai-Yangshan multilayered gateway hub. *Journal of Transport Geography, 25,* 58–69.

Williamson, O. E. (1979). Transaction-cost economics: The governance of contractual relations. *Journal of Law and Economics, 22,* 233–261.

Williamson, O. E. (1996). *The mechanisms of governance.* Oxford: Oxford University Press.

3

The Persistent Relevance of Transborder (Focal) Regions: The Case of the European Blue Banana

Paul Brugman and Alain Verbeke

1 Introduction

How much do borders matter? National governments and international organizations have done much to reduce the artificial barriers that impede trade and other cross-border flows, but are we yet in a position where borders can be considered inconsequential, at least in an economic sense? The impact of decreased border obstacles will likely be most pronounced for firms in former border areas, who are confronted with markets, competitors, and other influences from which the border previously insulated

P. Brugman (✉)
KBC Bank and Insurance, Brussels, Belgium

A. Verbeke
Haskayne School of Business, University of Calgary, Calgary, AB, Canada
e-mail: alain.verbeke@haskayne.ucalgary.ca

Department of Business, Vrije Universiteit Brussel, Brussels, Belgium

Henley Business School, University of Reading, Reading, UK

E. Haezendonck and A. Verbeke (eds.), *Sustainable Port Clusters and Economic Development*, Palgrave Studies in Maritime Economics,
https://doi.org/10.1007/978-3-319-96658-8_3

them. Among these influences are technological and economic spillover effects, which may become more pronounced as the border no longer poses an impenetrable barrier. In border regions, the removal of obstacles at borders could lead to cross-border homogenization such that both profit from integration, or both lose as economic activity relocates to other "core" regions. It is also possible though that one such region becomes a "core" region and acts as a magnet to attract economic activities from the other region, leading to an increased divergence between the two regions.

The research question thus can be framed in the broader dialectics of homogenization in the spirit of Levitt (1983) or persistent and relevant heterogeneity in the spirit of Ghemawat (2001). In this chapter, we compare and contrast two border regions that have been part of the European integration process since its very beginning and determine whether and to what extent differences exist from a firm's point of view. Ultimately, we are interested in whether unification has induced the formation of a single industrial region. We therefore commence our analysis with a short overview of the literature pertaining to industrial regions. The section thereafter introduces the extended diamond of Porter as the method used to analyze the regions. After this theoretical discussion, we turn to the actual analysis and discuss the results. We end with a short summary and conclusions.

2 Location Theory

The location of economic activity in general, and the individual firm by extension, is a much researched topic in the fields of economics and business. Among the pioneers in the field was Marshall, who analyzed the collocation of firms in specialized industries as early as the 1890s. The tendency of firms to agglomerate has attracted continuous attention since then (Krugman 1991, 1998; Fujita and Thisse 1996; Ottaviano and Puga 1998; Fujita et al. 1999; Malmberg and Maskell 1997; Neary 2001; Ottaviano and Thisse 2003). Even today prestigious journals feature multiple articles devoted to this topic. In addition to issues concerning where firms locate and for what reason, considerable attention has been devoted to the impact of this investment on both the firm and the recipient locale. *Ceteris paribus* firms are generally attracted to locations where other firms are already present due to the perceived advantages of a larger and deeper pool of employees, a larger availability of specialists and/or specialized inputs and possibilities to learn from competitors. In addition, Saxenian (1994) and Lucas (1988) emphasize the importance of personal communication in the spread of new knowledge, especially if this knowledge is tacit and non-codified. A similar argument can be found in Kogut and Zander (1992) who state that the transfer of tacit knowledge requires frequent interaction in small groups. At the same time, however, an ever larger presence of firms increases various costs (such as rents, wages, and various other congestion costs) and may lead to more intense competition. Such factors act as a counter-force to the tendency toward agglomeration. The extent to which agglomeration remains beneficial thus remains theoretically indeterminate. As Krugman (1991: 485) points out, a priori we do not know "How far does a technological spill-over spill?"

In their extensive review of the agglomeration literature, McCann and Folta (2008: 541) note that empirical researchers have often simply assumed de facto that agglomeration economies end at political borders, whether they be municipal, state/provincial or national, and that clusters of firms can therefore be taken to coincide with political or administrative units. They note that researchers who have not made this assumption have reported various empirical results, which taken together seem to suggest that how rapidly externalities diminish varies with the nature of the externality (e.g., knowledge spillovers versus the impact of greater access to specialized labor or other resources). Pe'er et al. (2008) provide another summary of such research (pp. 122–123) and then empirically test the distance to which different types of externalities extend as part of their study of de novo entry into Canadian manufacturing. They find that the impact of agglomeration economies in production and demand ends after about 5 miles (8 km), while the effects of competitive market structure and deterrence are confined to about 20 miles (32 km). The effect of asset turnover (a proxy for the market for used assets) extends the furthest, reaching out to 50 miles (80 km).

Certainly, the assumption made in much of the published research that externalities and therefore clusters end at borders should not be automatic. Administrative regions and their boundaries are a product of history and do not always (if ever) correspond to the economic reality of cross-border agglomerations or regional integration due to trade and investment flows (Amin and Thrift 1995; Thisse 2000). Indeed, the so-called double diamond modification of Porter's uni-national diamond, through which firms may benefit from the favorable conditions available in neighboring countries, is explicitly based on the idea that clusters may extend across borders (see, e.g., Rugman and D'Cruz 1993; Moon et al. 1995, 1998). In a similar vein, a specialized region does not exist separately from its national or supranational environment (Amin and Thrift 1992 as cited in Heidenreich 1998). However, borders are still a reality that businessmen and policymakers cannot ignore, and we should recognize that not all are equal (compare, e.g., the border between North and South Korea with that between the USA and Canada). Whether a particular border should serve as the boundary of a cluster is an empirical matter every bit as much as the number of miles or kilometers that a given type of externality may extend in the absence of any border. The residual power of borders as barriers to economic integration and the specific issues that continue to prevent complete unity become especially important in locations such as Europe, where enormous political and economic effort has been dedicated to the reduction of the obstacles posed by national borders in order to facilitate the cross-border flow of goods and ideas over an increasingly larger area.

3 The Selection of East Flanders/Zeeland as a Study Site

In this chapter, we confine ourselves to a single, albeit crucial element: the notion of differences and obstacles between adjacent regions in different countries. Put differently: rather than researching where exactly clusters end, we try to establish whether country borders have an impact on the cross-border operations of firms if both regions would otherwise seem likely to be part of the same cluster. The implications of this chapter for further cluster research are obvious: If national borders do have an impact, further research on clusters will have a reliable "extreme boundary" to work with. In addition, attention can then focus on the survival chances of clusters in small countries, and what policymakers can or should do to overcome the obstacle of a national border. If, on the other hand, national borders are found to have no or negligible impact on the cross-border operations of firms, attention should be more focused on the reach and geographical limits of technical externalities and how these might be affected by various policy measures. In addition, the implication of cross-border agglomerations means that policymakers from different governments will be affected by changes in the cluster, which could induce more cross-border cooperation.

Between the autumn of 2005 and spring 2006, we surveyed 101 firms in two adjacent regions in Europe to determine whether, and to what extent these two administrative regions can be considered a single economic region. The regional (provincial) Chambers of Commerce selected the firms in each region, whereby it should be noted that all respondents expressed an interest in cross-border cooperation to improve the firm's competitive position. The active participation of each Chamber of Commerce followed our request to have a sample of at least 50 companies in each region, providing adequate representation of the overall perceptions of the business environment by the private sector. The Chambers participated within the context of an EU-funded INTERREG project for which we provided the intellectual rationale, as outlined above. Incidentally, the INTERREG programme is an EU-funded program with the explicit goal to foster cross-border economic and social interactions. We developed a questionnaire, which was then administered by a high-level administrator of each Chamber of Commerce. The individuals interviewed were typically the CEO or a senior vice president with full knowledge of the firm's competitive strengths and the challenges/opportunities provided by the regional environment for business.

The cross-border region in question consists of the provinces of East Flanders (Belgium) and Zeeland (The Netherlands), both of which are part of the so-called blue banana. This blue banana is a corridor that stretches from "Lancashire (in Great Britain) to Tuscany (in Italy) with the highest population densities and cities, the highest value added per square kilometre and the highest traffic density in Europe" (Brunet 2002, translation ours). This concentration of economic power in a

European core region is dated as early as the ninth century by some authors (Therborn 1995: 194 in Heidenreich 1998) and is believed likely to retain its position as a core region for many years to come (Amin and Thrift 1995; Heidenreich 1998; Hospers 2002). Although some authors question the empirical validity of the banana (see Taylor and Hoyler 2000 for an overview), the same paper acknowledges the existence of a central European core where most important cities (defined as advanced services center) are located. Empirical support for the banana can be found in Amin and Thrift (1995), Heidenreich (1998), and Puga (2002) who find that this central region is characterized by significantly higher GDP per capita and lower unemployment than adjacent, non-core regions.

We hypothesize that the location of a firm within the banana is irrelevant for location advantages. Unless a firm wants to be present in a specific knowledge cluster (such as the Swiss watch industry), a firm simply chooses between locating within or outside of this banana. In this chapter, we analyze the location characteristics of two adjacent regions in the heart of the blue banana to determine whether these regions differ, if so to what extent, and how much these differences matter to the competitive advantage of local firms and the location advantage of these regions. Thus, in this chapter, we compare the local diamonds of East Flanders and Zeeland to determine their competitiveness and their relative strengths and weaknesses.

4 Background/General Description of the Dataset

If we wish to rigorously examine whether the borders matter, the ideal site for a study is where one might expect that they would not (obviously a border between hostile states or between two very different countries matters and would not represent much of a test). For this reason, we chose two border regions in North Western Europe: East Flanders in Belgium and Zeeland in The Netherlands. These two adjacent administrative regions in North Western Europe share the river Scheldt to import and export goods by sea, while a 30-km canal connects the port of Ghent (East Flanders, Belgium) with the port of Terneuzen (Zeeland, The Netherlands). In addition to sharing waterways, the two nations share some common history as part of larger political entities such as the Burgundian Netherlands (from 1432 to 1581), the French Empire in the 1800s and as single nation from 1815 to 1830. Furthermore, the Belgian and Dutch firms in this small cross-border region[1] share a common language (Dutch) and since 1999 a common currency (the euro). The industrial profile of both regions is characterized by a strong presence of the metal, chemical, and logistics sectors. Industrial services are also a significant activity in both. Although more than 70% of the firms visited have their national headquarters in the same region, 75% also were part of an international group. However, in 40% of the cases in East Flanders and 50% of the cases in Zeeland, the visited firm functioned as the global headquarters of such a group. As such, almost half of the firms in our sample could autonomously decide whether to cooperate or not. Respondents were also asked to name their top 3 export and import locations and the results reveal that the two regions are to a large extent similar, although more so with respect to exports than imports. Regarding exports, the home nation was most important (named over 30 times), while somewhat surprisingly the other nation (The Netherlands in case of East Flanders and Belgium in case of Zeeland) was not the second most named. Rather, France and Germany were tied for second place while The Netherlands and Belgium were ranked third. This result is most likely due to the much larger size of these nearby markets. Differences in export destination only appeared for the lower-ranked markets: the UK was named more often by firms from Zeeland, which were also the only ones to specifically identify Eastern Europe as important. Firms from East Flanders, on the other hand, specifically identified Spain. With respect to import sources, again the home nation was named most often, although The Netherlands was named considerably more often for firms from Zeeland than Belgium was named for firms from East Flanders. Flemish firms

[1]It takes 2 hours to travel by car from the north of Zeeland to the south of East Flanders.

ranked Germany second and The Netherlands as third most important import source, while Zeeland's firms ranked Belgium second and Germany as third most important source. Summarizing then, we can state that despite some minor differences, it is clear that the two regions are quite similar economically and culturally. In addition, trade relations are prevalent and virtually all firms have an international orientation.

Finally, these two provinces were chosen since both nations involved are part of the so-called blue banana and as founding members of the European Union share a 50-year history of European integration, and trade liberalization and deepening. Both home countries are part of the Schengen area, which has gone further than almost anywhere else on earth to remove border obstacles (border crossings within the Schengen area are marked by little more than a sign). At the local level, the ports of Ghent and Terneuzen have also signed an agreement to try to increase cooperation on various issues. In short, given their similarities and extensive history of removing the obstacles posed by the national border that divides them, this pairing provides an excellent example to study the residual powers, if any, of borders to differentiate neighboring regions. If borders still matter even here, then we ignore them elsewhere at our peril.

In the first part of this chapter, we construct diamonds of competitive forces for East Flanders and Zeeland to determine their strengths and weaknesses based on the work of Porter (1990a, b) and Moon et al. (1995, 1998). In total, we construct three such diamonds: one based on local endowment, one on importance perceived by firms, and one based on the combined scores.

5 Methodology

Before we turn to our first analysis, we present our methodology. Although regional analysis can be carried out in various ways (e.g., gravity analysis based on trade flows), the requirements the data must meet are often unattainable in the European context, especially if a comparison is made at the regional rather than national level (see also Combes and Overman 2004 on the quality of European data). In addition, in this chapter we chose to focus on the *perceptions* of managers with respect to local and interregional issues, since it is perceptions that will shape their actions most directly. Information on perceptions was unavailable in databases and therefore had to be gathered by the survey method. The survey itself is mainly inspired by the work of Porter, whose contributions to cluster research and competitive advantage are both recent and substantial. In addition, his works have led to various criticisms and extensions (see, e.g., Rugman et al. 1995 and the special issue in *Management International Review*, 1993) which have allowed us to improve upon and expand the original framework.

According to Porter, the competitive advantage of nations results from the presence and interaction of four dimensions: factor conditions, demand conditions, related and supporting industries, and strategy, structure, and rivalry. Together with random chance and a rather passive government, this environment determines whether internationally competitive firms and industries will emerge. An important aspect of Porter's framework is its emphasis on the home nation and local, indigenous firms as drivers of national competitive advantage, with foreign firms and FDI thought to be less, or not at all, important. However, as noted by several scholars (Rugman and D'Cruz 1993; Moon et al. 1995, 1998), small open economies are not likely to possess all of these conditions if only domestic sources are taken into account. Put differently, without FDI or cross-border trade that acts as a substitute for missing local conditions, these countries may never develop competitive industries. In fact, in our survey 42 of our respondents are part of an international group with global headquarters outside Belgium or The Netherlands, many of whom are among the most capital and labor-intensive firms in the region. We therefore reject a strict home-nation orientation in favor of the (more realistic) argument that foreign and national firms both contribute to regional competitiveness.

Given this critical role of FDI and cross-border trade, we have endogenized the role of the government and included it as a fifth factor in our analysis. While the government in Porter's work is conceptually a motivator and supplier of basic functions such as education, as a dimension it is virtually nonexistent in the single diamond framework. This absence is puzzling since the only actor interested solely in national competitiveness and by extension welfare is in fact the government (Moon et al. 1995). Finally, it is exactly the government that is best positioned to improve FDI and cross-border trade between the home nation and abroad, thus improving local conditions. In fact, the government has three policy mechanisms by which it can do so: improving the permeability of borders, unlocking latent location-specific advantages (LSAs), and crafting new, related location-specific advantages (Van Den Bulcke et al. 2009). Improving the permeability of borders means that obstacles to trade and FDI should be minimized, if not removed altogether, to support and contribute to national competitiveness. The second policy mechanism mirrors Porter in that policy "succeeds only when working in tandem with favourable underlying conditions in the diamond" (Porter 1990a). Put differently, the government should build upon existing LSAs rather than trying to create entirely new ones that are not connected in any way to the local environment. The final policy area entails the development of new, supporting LSAs specifically selected to complement and augment the firm-specific advantages of (foreign) firms. Not only will these LSAs improve local and national competitiveness, they will also improve the attractiveness of the country as an investment location while simultaneously increasing the barrier to divest. As a result, foreign activities become locked-in, or embedded in the national economic framework. It should be noted that the second and third policies are not contradictory, as the second cautions against developing unrelated LSAs, while the third encourages the creation of related LSAs.

Taking the double diamond approach and the activist government approach together, we can visualize the difference between our model and Porter's in Table 1.

The first column depicts Porter's traditional four-factor diamond while the three policies listed across the top represent the government as a fifth factor. Porter implies that the impact of these policies is weak at best. In this chapter and elsewhere (e.g., Moon et al. 1995), however, it is argued that the impact of these policies is in fact strong, especially when small, open economies are concerned; we have therefore shaded the right-hand portion of each column to highlight what we have added to Porter's model.

Table 1 Porter's diamond improved

	Improving permeability of borders		Unlocking latent location advantages		Crafting new location advantages	
	Weak	Strong	Weak	Strong	Weak	Strong
Factor conditions						
Demand conditions						
Related and supporting industries						
Strategy, structure and rivalry						

In our survey, 39 questions related to five of the six dimensions in Porters' framework (chance was obviously left out) were posed to 51 firms in East Flanders and 50 in Zeeland. Each respondent was asked to rate both the local endowment of—and importance attached to—each item. All questions required an answer on a 7-point scale where a score below 4 always indicates a degree of shortage, whereas a score above 4 indicates a degree of abundance.[2] A score of 4 is always the "neutral" answer. A preliminary analysis of the data revealed two noteworthy issues. First, due to the fact that firms from different industries were interviewed, not all questions were equally applicable to all respondents. As a result, 223 times for the "endowment" part of each question and 95 times for the "importance" part of each question, the answer "not relevant," "I do not know," or "I cannot disclose this information" was given.[3] These cases have been designated simply as "missing variables." As a result, we have 3945 observations with respect to the importance part of each question, and 3817 observations with respect to the endowment part. Given our relatively small dataset (50 and 51 firms per region) and the restricted range of responses, the data were subjected to a nonparametric analysis. Specifically, we used a Kolmogorov–Smirnoff analysis which allows us to compare the cumulative frequency distributions of the responses from both regions. Parallel to this analysis, a statistically weaker analysis was carried out through contingency tables, whereby we created two new categories by merging response categories 1, 2, 3, (low) and 5, 6, 7 (high), respectively. Category 4 was dropped from this analysis as it represents the "neutral" response and as such is less suitable when we are interested in differences between regions. In addition, allocating this category to either group would artificially inflate that group's results. The resulting 2 groups were then analyzed through contingency tables. A Pearson Chi-square test was used to determine significant differences. This way, we

[2]Degree of shortage is for example "low probability," "low importance," and "low dependency". Degree of abundance is for example "high probability," "high importance," and "high dependency".

[3]The missing variables were split 207—101 between East Flanders and Zeeland. For more information with respect to missing variables, the reader is referred to Table A2.2.

Table 2 Porter's diamond

Item	Factor conditions	Demand conditions	Related and supporting industries	Strategy, structure and rivalry	Government
Presence of important raw materials/inputs	x				
Availability of highly educated labour	x				
Availability of low educated labour	x				
Low cost of energy	x				
Low cost of information	x				
Presence telecom infrastructure	x				
Presence transport infrastructure (road, water, rail, air)	x				
Proximity of airport/seaport	x				
Access to financial institutions/capital	x				
Availability of land for expansion	x				
Attractive prices land / property	x				
Local presence of technology	x				
Good climate R&D	x				
Presence of institutions for higher education	x				
Quality of education and health care	x				
Relations/cooperation with knowledge institutions	x				
Presence of recreation/culturally important environment	x				
General quality of the envionment	x				
Tolerance and cultural diversity	x				
Prestige of the location	x			x	
Proximity of strategically important demand		x			

(continued)

Table 2 (continued)

Item	Factor conditions	Demand conditions	Related and supporting industries	Strategy, structure and rivalry	Government
Growth potential of strategically important demand		x			
Low wages		–			
Presence of constructive stakeholders		x			
Presence of big firms (competitors/ clients)		x	x	x	
Presence of many small firms (competitors/ clients)		x	x	x	
Presence of important suppliers			x		
Relations/ cooperation with local firms			x		
Local network/ social ties management in the region			x		
Local presence similar firms			x	x	
Historic success region				x	
Attractive work environment w.r.t. labour laws/unions					–
Political stability					x
Efficient government					x
Favorable policy/support w.r.t. location or expansion					–
Favorable tax rates and related regulations					–
Member of a tradebloc					x
Favorable corporate regulations					–
Degree of openness/internationalisation of the region					x

could test specifically for significant differences between the two regions with respect to their overall orientation (more negative or more positive than the other). However, as most results are identical to those obtained in the Kolmogorov–Smirnoff analysis, only deviations will be reported in the text.

The table provides an overview of the allocation of each item in our survey to the 5 dimensions. The minus (−) signs indicate a negative relation between the individual item and the creation of competitive advantage. In addition, some items (specifically those related to the presence of firms) were allocated to multiple dimensions, as firms sometimes combine various roles in a region. For example, large firms can exert demand, can be part of related and supporting industries, and can influence the strategy and structure of other firms in the region. For the sake of completeness, these items were allocated to all relevant dimensions. After allocating the individual items to their respective dimensions, we carry out an item-by-item comparison. The final step in the analysis is the construction of the diamonds of both regions, as in Moon et al. (1995, 1998) (Table 2).

6 Factor Conditions

According to Porter (1990a: 74), factor conditions consist of human, physical, knowledge and capital resources, and infrastructure. The allocation of most of the items from our dataset is self-explanatory, with the exception perhaps of "relations/cooperation with knowledge institutions," this item was included in the dimension "factor conditions," as "*Competitive advantage from factors depends on how efficiently and effectively they are deployed*" (Porter 1990a: 76; emphasis his). Thus, in addition to the "presence of institutions of higher education," we also need to take account of how much use is made of them. Put differently, the existence of a knowledge infrastructure itself does not necessarily induce or improve competitive advantage.[4]

[4]Although, as noted above, Porter argues that education is a government concern he considers the knowledge infrastructure to be a factor condition.

Table 3 provides an overview of the median item endowment scores as we are, for now, interested in the actual condition of the local diamond rather than the importance attached to the individual items. Next to each item's median[5] we find the Kolmogorov–Smirnoff results. We focus our discussion on items that differ significantly between the regions and those items where either region scores below 4, as indicated in bold.[6] Both regions are well endowed with respect to factor conditions, the sole exception is the item "low cost of energy" where both regions (and especially East Flanders) score at or below average (defined here as an overall score of 4 or below). Although this result is not too surprising in a Western-European context, the fact that both regions face this issue could perhaps induce future cooperation in this regard. This incentive would be especially large in case a solution is sufficiently footloose. Turning to the Kolmogorov–Smirnoff results, we observe that the regions report significantly different results for 7 items. Whereas Zeeland scores better with respect to the availability of land and price of land and property, and the general quality of the environment, East Flanders has a significantly better educational, medical, and cultural infrastructure, and an overall higher prestige. Of final note is the item "relations/cooperation with knowledge institutions," where Chi-square results reveal a significant difference[7]; a quarter of the respondents in Zeeland gave this item low score (3 or below) compared to 3 cases in East Flanders. As such, we can conclude that East Flanders seems significantly better endowed, at the very least for a large subgroup. In summary then, while "basic" factor conditions necessary for the normal, day-to-day operations of a firm, the two regions are (statistically) almost identical; there are a number of differences in the social and economic infrastructure. Since such matters are largely within the purview of governments to determine through their policy choices, in principle it is possible to reduce or eliminate these differences if the political will to do so exists.

[5]Due to the ordinal nature of the data only median scores will be reported.

[6]At the 10% level.

[7]At the 1% level.

Table 3 Factor conditions (endowment)

Endowment—Factor conditions	Median		Kolmogorov–Smirnoff	
Item	Flanders	Zeeland	Value	Assymp. Sig (2-sided)
Presence of important raw materials/inputs	4.0	5.0	.314	1.000
Availability of higher educated labor	5.0	4.5	.620	.837
Availability of lower educated labor	4.0	5.0	1.072	.201
Low cost of energy	**3.0**	4.0	.523	.947
Low cost of information	6.0	6.0	.203	1.000
Presence telecom infrastructure	7.0	6.0	1.200	.112
Presence transport infrastructure (road, water, rail, air)	6.0	6.0	.579	.891
Proximity of airport/ seaport	6.0	6.0	.516	.953
Access to financial institutions/capital	6.0	6.0	.492	.969
Availability of land for expansion	4.0	6.0	1.701	**.006**
Attractive prices land/ property	4.0	5.0	2085	**.000**
Local presence of technology	5.0	5.0	.544	.928
Good climate R&D	5.0	5.0	.483	.974
Presence of institutions for higher education	6.0	5.0	2.094	**.000**
Quality of education and health care	6.0	5.0	2.030	**.001**
Relations/cooperation with knowledge institutions	6.0	5.0	1.021	.249
Presence of recreation/ culturally important environment	6.0	5.0	1.400	**.040**
General quality of the environment	5.0	6.0	1.500	**.022**
Tolerance and cultural diversity	5.0	5.0	.392	.998
Prestige of the location	5.0	4.0	1.484	**.024**

7 Demand Conditions

The second dimension in Porter's diamond framework is demand, split into three different, interacting parts: composition, size, and internationalization (Porter 1990a: 86). Thus, we included all items that dealt with demand directly or indirectly (e.g., the presence of big and small firms). In addition, "presence of constructive stakeholders" was included, as their needs and feedback may induce a firm to innovate or improve operations. Finally, the scores for "low wages" were reversed in that a score of 1 became 7, 2 became 6, etc. The reason is that according to Porter, higher wages allow consumers more choice and allow them to be more critical of the products they buy, which in turn may induce more innovation within the firm. Related to this reasoning is that a higher income makes innovative products affordable.

Table 4 reveals that East Flanders is relatively better endowed with respect to demand conditions. Not only is the region better endowed with respect to proximate strategic demand, wages are also higher. Finally, though not significantly different, Zeeland scores below average with respect to the growth potential of demand. The results reported in Table 4 are somewhat surprising since given the very compact nature of the combined region (whose total area is smaller than some

Table 4 Demand conditions (endowment)

Endowment—Demand conditions	Median		Kolmogorov–Smirnoff	
Item	Flanders	Zeeland	Value	Assymp. Sig (2-sided)
Proximity of strategically important demand	6.0	4.0	1.466	**.027**
Growth potential of strategically important demand	4.0	**3.0**	.581	.889
Low wages	4.0	**3.0**	1.633	**.010**
Presence of constructive stakeholders	5.0	5.0	.600	.864
Presence of big firms (competitors/clients)	5.0	5.0	.388	.998
Presence of many small firms (competitors/clients)	5.0	5.5	.318	1.000

of the world's major metropolitan agglomerations) one might have expected that demand and labor prices would be more homogeneous. Apparently, no or little arbitrage occurs between the two regions.

8 Related and Supporting Industries

Both related and supporting industries may confer competitive advantage to firms in their surroundings through coordination throughout the value chain and world-class output, respectively (Porter 1990a: 104). As a result, we included all factors that dealt with the presence of firms and their interaction as in Table 5. Although some of these items have been discussed above, they were included again to provide insight into this specific factor of Porter's diamond.

Table 5 reveals that the two regions score moderately well and do not differ significantly with the exception of the "local presence of similar firms," where East Flanders scores significantly better. However, it should be noted that these measures of cooperation and interaction seem to be primarily local, rather than interregional. Since, next to the asking after the endowment and importance of various items, also included in the survey was the question that "Indicate, on

Table 5 Related and supporting industries (endowment)

Endowment—Related and supporting industries	Median		Kolmogorov–Smirnoff	
Item	Flanders	Zeeland	Value	Assymp. Sig (2-sided)
Presence of big firms (competitors/clients)	5.0	5.0	.388	.998
Presence of many small firms (competitors/clients)	5.0	5.5	.318	1.000
Presence of important suppliers	4.0	5.0	.765	.602
Relations/cooperation with local firms	6.0	5.5	.568	.904
Local network/social ties management in the region	6.0	6.0	.686	.734
Local presence similar firms	5.0	4.0	1.225	**.100**

the basis of a 7-point Likert scale (ranging from not at all to excellent) how well East Flanders and Zeeland operate as a unified region." The response was overwhelmingly negative with a median score of 2. Moreover, only 17.20% of the respondents indicated that East Flanders and Zeeland operate well or very well (scores 5 and 6) as a unified region. Although more respondents in Zeeland were positive than those from East Flanders (22% versus 12, 20%), this difference is not significant.

9 Strategy, Structure, and Rivalry

The fourth component of Porter's diamond consists of firm strategy, structure, and rivalry. No strategy or way of management is universal, and according to Porter firms succeed if an optimal match can be found between an industry's competitive advantages and the national environment (Porter 1990a: 108). Rivalry is considered to be among the more (if not most) important factors affecting competitive advantage, as "Competitive advantage emerges from pressure, challenge and adversity…" (Porter 1990a: 174). In addition, it is argued that geographic proximity increases the pressure of rivalry by making it both more personal and more relevant since a proximate similar firm makes use of the same pool of resources, thus eliminating the excuse that competitors profit from an unfair (local) advantage. As noted above, with the exception of "historic success," all items in this dimension have been discussed. As such, only "prestige" and "local presence similar firms" differ significantly between the regions.

The last two dimensions in Porter's framework are chance and the government. For obvious reasons, chance was not included in our survey, while Porter suggests the role of the government should merely be to support a healthy competitive environment. However, in Moon et al. (1995) it is suggested that the government should actually be seen as a fifth factor in Porter's model, and should be placed in the center of the diamond (Moon et al. 1995: 111). Following this line of reasoning, the government as a fifth factor is analyzed below.

10 Government

The government, in Porter's diamond, affects all the dimensions above and can do so positively or negatively. "Government's proper role is as a catalyst and challenger..." (Porter 1990b: 86). Generally speaking, the more difficult the local environment (within reasonable bounds), the more firms will be forced to innovate, which in turn allows firms to compete much more successfully abroad. In fact, the literature on innovation and competition has advanced the idea of an inverted U-shaped relationship between these two variables (Aghion et al. 2005). Our dimension thus contains all factors pertaining to government action. Stability, efficient government, openness, and membership of a trade bloc are all considered to have a positive impact on competitiveness while favorable regulations are considered to have a negative impact. Put differently, the task of the government is to provide an environment conducive to business, i.e., where the market fully functions. Therefore, we have reversed the item scores that explicitly ask after favorable regulations (see Table 1) so that 1 = 7, etc.

Table 6 reveals that the scores for this dimension vary somewhat and although lower than the other dimensions are sufficient overall, with an attractive work environment as a notable exception. Thus, respondents from both regions found that their work environment was quite attractive

Table 6 Government scores (endowment)

Endowment—Government	Median		Kolmogorov–Smirnoff	
Item	Flanders	Zeeland	Value	Assymp. Sig (2-sided)
Attractive work environment w.r.t. labor laws/unions	**3.0**	**3.0**	.645	.800
Political stability	5.0	5.5	.772	.590
Efficient government	4.0	4.0	.600	.864
Favorable policy/support w.r.t. location or expansion	4.0	**3.0**	.768	.597
Favorable tax rates and related regulations	4.0	**3.0**	1.713	**.006**
Member of a trade bloc	6.0	7.0	.707	.699
Favorable corporate regulations	4.0	4.0	.430	.993
Degree of openness/internationalization of the region	5.5	4.0	1.192	.117

regarding labor laws and unions, which indicates little pressure on firms. In addition, with respect to policy support for expansion and tax issues, Zeeland is more forthcoming than East Flanders, significantly so regarding taxes. Further, Zeeland scores significantly better with respect to political stability, while East Flanders is considered slightly more open.

Having compared the individual items within each dimension, we now turn to constructing a diamond for each of the two regions by making use of the methodology in Moon et al. (1998). Thus, for each dimension a so-called dimensional competitiveness index is constructed according to the following formula:

$$I_{d,j} = \left(\frac{\sum_{i(d)} \frac{\alpha_{i(d),j}}{\max_{j} \alpha_{i(d),j}}}{n_d} \right) \times 100 \qquad (1)$$

Where I is the dimensional competitiveness index, d denotes the individual dimension, j denotes the region, i denotes the item, and α denotes the median item score as presented in the tables. The index ranges from 14.3 to 100, where the former indicates that one region has a score of 1 for all items of that dimension while the other has a score of 7. A score of 100 indicates that a region scores equally well or higher for each item of that dimension. This index, therefore, does not indicate how well a region scores in general but only provides information as to how well one region scores relative to the other. As noted above, our diamonds are constructed with the government as a fifth factor.

Figure 1 reveals that overall neither region has a major advantage on any dimension, with the exception of demand conditions, where East Flanders scores much better. In addition, East Flanders is better endowed with respect to the government and strategy, structure and rivalry. However, these differences should not be exaggerated, as Zeeland still scores above 85 on each dimension, which indicates that the region scores as well, if not better on various individual items, as seen above. More interesting, therefore, are the differences in relative strengths and weaknesses. Whereas East Flanders obtains its highest score for demand conditions and its lowest on factor conditions, Zeeland scores best with respect to related and supporting industries

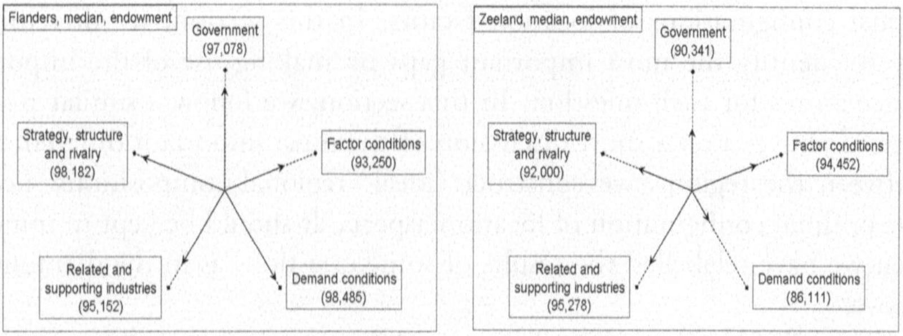

Fig. 1 Diamonds based on median scores (endowment)

and worst with respect to demand conditions. In addition, when comparing the dimensions individually no region dominates the other, i.e., surpasses it on all dimensions. Perhaps most surprising is the higher score for Zeeland regarding factor conditions since, as discussed above, East Flanders scores significantly better on various individual items. Also, the higher score for Zeeland with respect to related and supporting industries seems counterintuitive after the discussion above, although the relative scores do not differ much. Finally, summing the individual dimensional competitiveness indices while assuming that each dimension carries equal weight, East Flanders scores 96.43 while Zeeland scores 91.64. Overall, then, we can state that East Flanders is relatively better endowed than Zeeland, if only slightly so. In addition, the two are more like than unlike as only 15 of 39 items differed significantly. However, East Flanders generally scores better for items where a significant difference exists.

It would be premature, however, to proclaim that East Flanders is the stronger region, and that Zeeland will most likely lose from integration over the longer term. The analysis only focuses on how well the two regions are endowed and does not address whether what is offered by the regions is what is needed by the firms and vice versa. As a result, not all items will be equally important and neither can it be expected that the supply (endowment) and demand (importance) of all items will be in exact balance. Moreover, although the firms present in the two regions have invested there, or at least did not decide to relocate, a gap may well exist between the optimal (or desired) and actual configurations of location factors. In this section, we therefore try to identify the most important gaps by making use of the importance scores for each question. In this section, we follow a similar pattern as above; after a short discussion of the most important differences between the regions, we construct "ideal" regional compositions, i.e., the optimal configuration of location aspects. It should be kept in mind that we have relabelled the results of some questions as in the diamond above.

Table 7 identifies that the only difference between the regions lies with the importance associated with recreation and a culture in Zeeland. In addition, the Chi-square results reveal significant differences with respect to the presence of raw materials and the availability of land. In East Flanders, 40% of respondents discounted the importance of raw materials against 60% in Zeeland, which also explains the below average scores in the table. Regarding the availability of land, these percentages were 20% and 40%, respectively. Finally, we observe a low importance attached to financial institutions/capital; perhaps the excellent transportation infrastructure and communications in the region have lessened the importance of distance in these areas (Table 7).

With respect to demand conditions, see Table 8, it is clear that East Flanders attaches significantly more importance to the growth potential of demand and to some extent also its proximity. This latter result is confirmed by the Chi-square analysis that reveals a significant difference between the regions: Whereas almost 80% of respondents from Flanders value proximate demand, less than 60% do so in Zeeland. It should be noted, however, that respondents from Zeeland do significantly differ with their counterpart from East Flanders regarding the presence of small firms; 70%, respectively, 50% found this issue to be somewhat to very important. Thus, although Zeeland is not indifferent to demand conditions, it is clear that East Flanders is more preoccupied with this issue. The low score for high wages (low wages recoded) therefore seems somewhat surprising. It may indicate that firms from both regions are more active in a business-to-business rather than a business-to-consumer environment. Support for this hypothesis can be found with the high scores attached to the presence of big and small firms, especially so in case of Zeeland.

Table 7 Factor conditions (importance)

Importance—Factor conditions	Median		Kolmogorov–Smirnoff	
Item	Flanders	Zeeland	Value	Assymp. Sig (2-sided)
Presence of important raw materials/inputs	**3.0**	**2.0**	1.015	.254
Availability of higher educated labor	5.0	5.0	.745	.635
Availability of lower educated labor	6.0	6.0	.958	.318
Low cost of energy	6.0	6.0	.730	.661
Low cost of information	6.0	6.0	.473	.979
Presence telecom infrastructure	6.0	6.0	.600	.864
Presence transport infrastructure (road, water, rail, air)	7.0	7.0	1.031	.239
Proximity of airport/seaport	6.0	6.0	.400	.997
Access to financial institutions/ capital	**3.0**	4.0	.798	.548
Availability of land for expansion	6.0	5.0	.800	.544
Attractive prices land/property	5.5	6.0	.553	.919
Local presence of technology	4.0	5.0	.700	.711
Good climate R&D	4.0	5.0	.828	.499
Presence of institutions for higher education	5.5	6.0	.300	1.000
Quality of education and health care	6.0	6.0	.201	1.000
Relations/cooperation with knowledge institutions	5.0	4.0	.581	.889
Presence of recreation/culturally important environment	4.0	6.0	1957	**.001**
General quality of the environment	6.0	6.0	1.000	.270
Tolerance and cultural diversity	5.0	5.0	.534	.938
Prestige of the location	5.0	5.0	.459	.984

In Table 9, we observe again high scores with respect to the business-to-business environment. However, Zeeland attaches virtually no importance to either the presence of suppliers or similar firms in contrast to respondents from East Flanders.

As indicated above, the dimension strategy, structure, and rivalry does not contain other items but the historic success of the region, and as above, no significant difference exists between the regions.

Table 8 Demand conditions (importance)

Importance—Demand conditions	Median		Kolmogorov–Smirnoff	
Item	Flanders	Zeeland	Value	Assymp. Sig (2-sided)
Proximity of strategically important demand	6.0	4.5	1.200	.112
Growth potential of strategically important demand	6.0	5.0	1.253	**.087**
Low wages	**2.0**	**2.0**	.479	.976
Presence of constructive stakeholders	6.0	6.0	.575	.895
Presence of big firms (competitors/clients)	6.0	6.0	.272	1.000
Presence of many small firms (competitors/clients)	5.0	6.0	.975	.297

Table 9 Related and supporting industries (importance)

Importance—Related and supporting industries	Median		Kolmogorov–Smirnoff	
Item	Flanders	Zeeland	Value	Assymp. Sig (2-sided)
Presence of big firms (competitors/clients)	6.0	6.0	.272	1.000
Presence of many small firms (competitors/clients)	5.0	6.0	.975	.297
Presence of important suppliers	5.0	**3.0**	.681	.742
Relations/cooperation with local firms	6.0	6.0	.296	1.000
Local network/social ties management in the region	6.0	6.0	.252	1.000
Local presence similar firms	4.0	**2.0**	1.006	.263

Two important observations can be made with respect to the government. The first is that all recoded variables have a median score of 2, which implies that our respondents were virtually unanimous in the importance attached to government support. This in turn implies that the government is valued as a partner rather than as a challenger. A second observation is that respondents from East Flanders attach significantly more importance to favorable tax rates and regulations than their counterparts from

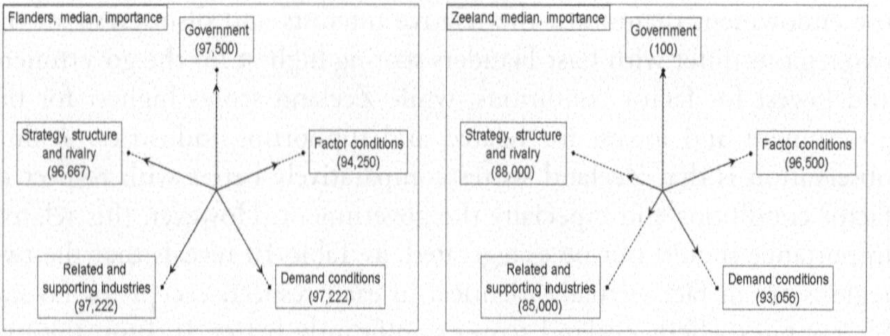

Fig. 2 Diamonds based on median scores (importance)

Table 10 Government

Importance—Government	Median		Kolmogorov–Smirnoff	
Item	Flanders	Zeeland	Value	Assymp. Sig (2-sided)
Attractive work environment w.r.t. labor laws/unions	**2.0**	**2.0**	.500	.964
Political stability	6.0	6.0	.670	.760
Efficient government	6.0	6.0	.500	.964
Favorable policy/support w.r.t. location or expansion	**2.0**	**2.0**	.664	.770
Favorable tax rates and related regulations	**2.0**	**2.5**	1324	**.060**
Member of a trade bloc	6.0	6.0	.600	.864
Favorable corporate regulations	**2.0**	**2.0**	.365	.999
Degree of openness/internationalization of the region	6.0	6.0	.199	1000

Zeeland.[8] Taking all these results together, and using Eq. (1), we can now construct optimal diamond configurations, as depicted (Fig. 2).

The diamonds above expose rather large differences between the two regions with respect to the importance associated with the various dimensions. A first observation is the discrepancy between East Flanders, whose dimension scores are more or less similar, and Zeeland, whose dimension scores vary more widely. Second, as with

[8]Given that favourable tax rates are a recoded variable, a lower score indicates that favourable tax rates are considered less important to the firm.

the endowment diamonds, the relative interests and disinterests of the two regions differ with East Flanders scoring highest for the government and lowest for factor conditions, while Zeeland scores highest for the government and lowest for related and supporting industries. A final observation is that Zeeland scores comparatively better with respect to factor conditions and especially the government. However, this relative importance should not be exaggerated, as Table 10 reveals that the two regions are in fact virtually identical in each respect, except for favorable tax rates where Zeeland scores significantly better. In sum, the two regions hardly differ with respect to their desires, as evidenced by only 6 significant item differences.

11 Opportunities to Improve Local Conditions

In an ideal world, the conditions available to firms would exactly match what they needed, with no resources expended providing unnecessary conditions and none spared where their provision was economically rational. How close does this region come to the ideal? We examine this question by first dividing the respondent's median endowment score per item by its respective importance score, to obtain new scores ranging from 1/7 to 7. The idea is that a score of 1, i.e., an item is equally valued as it is locally present, represents an optimal situation. Any deviation from this optimum results in scores that are either above 1, which indicates that a region is relatively better endowed than considered necessary, or in scores below 1 which indicates that a region is underendowed regarding that specific item. The latter may point to a problem (or competitive disadvantage) while the former could be exploited as a competitive advantage if it is valued by firms other than those currently in the location. The *table* provides a schematic.

In Table 11, importance scores can be found on the vertical axis while endowment scores can be found on the horizontal axis. Each score can be placed in one cell of this schematic. The shaded areas represent the optimal configurations as discussed above. Above this "optimal

Table 11 Distribution of item scores

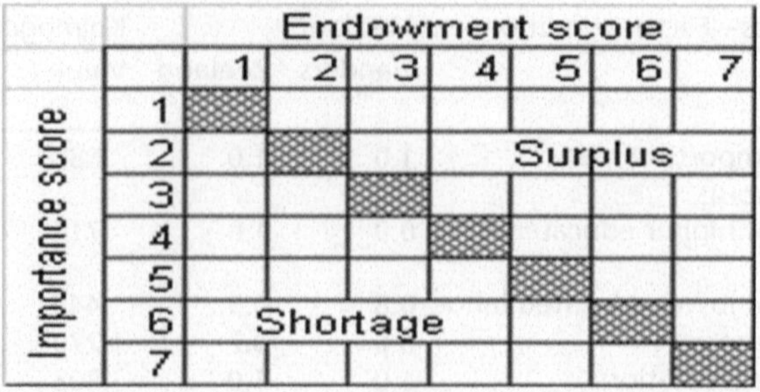

line," we find combinations where local endowment exceeds the importance placed on it by existing firms. These may be areas from which resources can be redeployed, or efforts targeted to attract firms that will value these characteristics. Finally, and perhaps most important to policymakers and firms alike, the area below the optimal line captures items where the region is underendowed. The items in this area represent competitive disadvantages in the region. As before, we first provide an overview of the median scores of the various items and the chi-square results. It should be noted that rather than comparing a high with a low group, in the following analysis we compare the surplus with the deficit group. Thus, all scores below 1 (endowment scores lower than importance) are allocated to the deficit group while scores above 1 are allocated to the surplus group.[9]

From Table 12, various observations can be made. The first is that although the regions differ significantly in 7 out of 20 respects, only 3 items could potentially be used to overcome a shortage in the other region. As such these represent opportunities for joint policy, especially regarding the low cost of energy which is the direct shortage faced by both regions. Other opportunities for cooperation lie with a shared shortage for lower educated labor and the transport infrastructure which at least in case of labor attraction would be desired due to the ease of crossing the border to work in the other region. Another

[9]Thus, all scores equal to 1, i.e., cases where a respondent indicates that an item is as present as desired are left out of the analysis.

Table 12 Divided scores for factor conditions

Divided scores—Factor conditions	Median		Kolmogorov–Smirnoff	
Item	Flanders	Zeeland	Value	Assymp. Sig (2-sided)
Presence of important raw materials/inputs	1.0	1.0	.888	.409
Availability of higher educated labor	**0.9**	1.0	.714	.687
Availability of lower educated labor	**0.8**	**0.9**	.449	.988
Low cost of energy	**0.6**	**0.7**	1.270	**.080**
Low cost of information	1.0	1.0	.808	.531
Presence telecom infrastructure	1.0	1.0	1.300	**.068**
Presence transport infrastructure (road, water, rail, air)	**0.9**	**0.9**	.774	.588
Proximity of airport/seaport	1.0	1.0	.516	.953
Access to financial institutions/ capital	1.2	1.3	.788	.564
Availability of land for expansion	1.0	1.2	1.680	**.007**
Attractive prices land/property	**0.8**	1.0	1.637	**.009**
Local presence of technology	1.0	1.0	1.097	.180
Good climate R&D	1.0	1.0	.966	.308
Presence of institutions for higher education	1.1	1.0	1.807	**.003**
Quality of education and health care	1.0	**0.8**	1.535	**.018**
Relations/cooperation with knowledge institutions	1.0	1.0	.598	.866
Presence of recreation/culturally important environment	1.5	1.0	2.900	**.000**
General quality of the environment	1.0	1.0	.500	.964
Tolerance and cultural diversity	1.0	1.0	.640	.807
Prestige of the location	1.0	1.0	1.148	.143

area of cross-border activity identified in the table is that of land and property, where Zeeland has both more land and (possibly as a result) more attractive prices. It is somewhat surprising that these differences are significant given a lack of formal barriers to economic activity in the European Union. As a result, here another opportunity exists for policymakers to cooperate, as location/expansion in Zeeland allows for additional growth that could spill over to the region as a whole. Finally, the Chi-square analysis revealed that the two regions differ significantly with respect to the presence of raw materials (identified by 20% of the respondents in East Flanders as a shortage versus 10% in Zeeland) and the presence of technology (a shortage according to 12% in East Flanders versus 40% in Zeeland). Although the latter observation seems to match with the observed significant deficit in Zeeland regarding health care and education, further research has revealed that Zeeland's identified deficit lies with the former rather than the latter. Since, as Zeeland is a rather low-density region, longer distances must be travelled to receive specialized care (Table 13).

With respect to demand, the regions face identical problems in the form of a lack of growth potential of demand and a lack of constructive stakeholders. Given that East Flanders has a significant surplus with respect to high wages; further support can be found for our earlier hypothesis that firms in our sample are especially active in a business-to-business environment. It is therefore important to both regions to attract/develop new demand in this segment, and again due to the possible lack of regional integration, greater cooperation may be in the best interest of all. With respect to the dimensions related and

Table 13 Divided scores for demand conditions

Divided scores—Demand conditions	Median		Kolmogorov–Smirnoff	
Item	Flanders	Zeeland	Value	Assymp. Sig (2-sided)
Proximity of strategically important demand	1.0	1.0	.777	.582
Growth potential of strategically important demand	**0.7**	**0.8**	.881	.420
Low wages	2.0	1.0	1.429	**.034**
Presence of constructive stakeholders	**0.9**	**0.8**	.500	.964
Presence of big firms (competitors/clients)	1.0	1.0	.348	1.000
Presence of many small firms (competitors/clients)	1.0	1.0	.883	.417

supporting industries, and strategy, structure and rivalry, no deficits were identified and the two regions did not differ significantly on any item. The respective tables are therefore omitted from this chapter.

Finally, the results of the fifth and last dimension are not very surprising and are in line with previous observations. Simply put: the governments in both regions are perceived as inefficient and too little forthcoming with respect to policy and regulations, especially in East Flanders. Although from a regional competition view a strict government may be desirable, the significant differences in regulatory environment could possibly induce relocation from East Flanders to Zeeland (especially given a lack of formal borders and the availability of attractively priced property) or a race to the bottom with all its undesirable side effects. Although cooperation would be infeasible in many areas due to national regulations, perhaps best practices can be exchanged. Finally, we note the significant deficit with respect to the openness of the region in Zeeland (Table 14).

Summarizing, perhaps the most surprising observation is that the two regions face nearly the same deficits, with nearly identical top 3 items, as shown below. The *table* was constructed by ranking all items with a score below 1, with the lowest score noted first and then descending (Table 15).

Table 14 Divided scores for government

Divided scores—Government				
Item	Flanders (Median)	Zeeland (Median)	Chi-square value	Probability (df: 1)
Attractive work environment w.r.t. labor laws/unions	1.50	1.33	2.901	**0.089**
Political stability	1.00	1.00	0.912	0.340
Efficient government	**0.69**	**0.67**	0.005	0.944
Favorable policy/support w.r.t. location or expansion	2.00	1.50	3.280	**0.070**
Favorable tax rates and related regulations	2.00	1.33	12.875	**0.000**
Member of a trade bloc	1.00	1.00	1.904	0.168
Favorable corporate regulations	2.50	2.00	0.793	0.373
Degree of openness/internationalization of the region	1.00	**0.83**	4.797	**0.029**

Table 15 Shared deficits

East Flanders	Zeeland
Low cost of energy	Efficient government
Efficient government	Low cost of energy
Growth potential of strategically important demand	Growth potential of strategically important demand
Availability of low educated labor	Presence of constructive stakeholders
Presence of transport infrastructure (road, water, rail, air)	Presence transport infrastructure (road, water, rail, air)
Presence of constructive stakeholders	Availability of low educated labor

12 Conclusion

In this chapter, we have established that East Flanders and Zeeland, two adjacent regions located in the European blue banana, are more like than unlike. However, from the perspective of business, a number of differences exist, many of which are in areas typically under direct government jurisdiction, such as social and physical infrastructure. Clearly these are areas where greater intergovernmental coordination could result in a lessening of perceived differences, assuming these differences are not important reflections of different local values in the two regional populations.

The continued importance of differences in competitive conditions between the two regions, whose border has become almost invisible, suggests that researchers must carefully consider the impact of borders, as well as simple physical distance, when studying externalities or the clusters to which they may give rise.

As for policymakers, when asked whether the two regions operate as a unified whole, the median score of respondents in both regions was 2. Thus, managers in either region do not support this proposition, despite decades of intergovernmental efforts to reduce the obstacles posed by barriers. This suggests that if we do want to see borders truly become irrelevant, high-level intergovernmental efforts need to be supplemented by greater coordination at the local level by both the public and private sectors. Managers, for example, could improve local conditions by exchanging best practices and pooling resources to try and attract new demand to the combined region (e.g., through joint presentations at investment fairs). If such local integration efforts are needed even in a region that seems otherwise so homogeneous, they are likely to be even more urgent where differences are greater.

Borders will continue to matter, it seems, until and unless deliberate efforts are made to identify and eliminate the last vestiges of their subtle and lingering influence.

13 Limitations and Directions for Future Research

This study suffers from 3 main limitations. First, although much effort was expended to contact the most important actors in both regions so as to gain sufficient insight into the nature of the interactions between the regions, our sample is relatively small precluding more in-depth analysis of the respondent's sentiments and perceptions. Second, in our analysis we make no distinction between firms based on their size or their nationality. That is, it may be that large, international or multinational enterprises in the region have different perceptions than those shared by smaller firms. For example, due to the former's experience in international affairs, local barriers may seem less daunting. Related to this observation, is that changes in ownership and especially changes in the nationality of the owners (e.g., Arcelor became part of an Indian conglomerate or Volvo that was acquired by a Chinese firm) may have a dramatic impact in how the region is perceived by the firm. A final shortcoming is that we did not address differences in the underlying rationale for investing in the region. That is, there are likely significant differences in perception between market-seeking purposes and resource-seeking firms.

In addition to these limitations, several other directions for future research can be identified. First, research into interregional clusters and cooperation is still rather limited. This is an important gap in our knowledge and addressing this issue would be welcome as many opportunities, both financial and other, can be unlocked if we understand why interregional cooperation does or does not occur. Second, the original research was carried out over 5 years ago and the region has seen substantial change since then. It may therefore be interesting to revisit respondents to determine whether, to what extent and in what way perceptions and endowments have changed if at all.

The reader may be interested to know that the study underlying this chapter has resulted in the creation of a cross-border organization that aims at fostering (further) cooperation between firms from East Flanders and Zeeland. Principal participants in this organization are the chambers of commerce of both regions and the employee organizations from both ports. One major aim of the organization is the development of a joint vision with regard to infrastructure and port-related issues. In the longer run, however, the organization aims at developing a cross-border master plan for the entire Canal Zone. Clearly, the participants feel that strength comes from unity, as evidenced by the subtitle of the first joint research document: "From disparate positions to more integration" (translated from Dutch). In the shorter term and in recognition of the existing lack of integration, however, various initiatives are being deployed to overcome information obstacles to operate in the other region. In addition, communication between firms is being fostered while a joint agenda of issues is being presented to policymakers in both regions.

References

Aghion, P., Bloom, N., Blundell, R., Griffith, R., & Howitt, P. (2005). Competition and innovation: An inverted-U relationship. *Quarterly Journal of Economics, 120*(2), 701–728.

Amin, A., & Thrift, N. (1992). Neo-Marshallian nodes in global networks. *International Journal of Urban and Regional Research, 16*, 571–587.

Amin, A., & Thrift, N. (1995). Institutional issues for the European regions: From markets and plans to socioeconomics and powers of association. *Economy and Society, 24*(1), 41–66.

Brunet, R. (2002). Lignes de force de l'espace Européen. *Mappe Monde, 66*(2), 14–19.

Combes, P.-P., & Overman, H. G. (2004). The spatial distribution of economic activities in the European Union. In V. Henderson & J. F. Thisse

(Eds.), *Handbook of regional and urban economics: Cities and geography*. North Holland: Elsevier.
Fujita, M., & Thisse, J.-F. (1996). Economics of agglomeration. *Journal of the Japanese and International Economies, 10*(4), 339–378.
Fujita, M., Krugman, P., & Venables, T. (1999). *The spatial economy—Cities, regions and international trade*. Cambridge: The MIT Press.
Ghemawat, P. (2001). Distance still matters: The hard reality of global expansion. *Harvard Business Review, 79*(8), 137–147.
Heidenreich, M. (1998). The changing system of European cities and regions. *European Planning Studies, 6*(3), 315–333.
Hospers, G.-J. (2002). Beyond the blue banana? Structural change in Europe's geo-economy. *Intereconomics: Review of European Economic Policy, 38*(2), 76–85.
Kogut, B., & Zander, U. (1992). Knowledge of the firm, combinative capabilities, and the replication of technology. *Organization Science, 3*(3), 383–397.
Krugman, P. (1991). Increasing returns and economic geography. *Journal of Political Economy, 99*(3), 483–499.
Krugman, P. (1998). What is new about the new economic geography? *Oxford Journal of Economic Policy, 14*(2), 7–17.
Levitt, T. (1983). The globalization of markets. *Harvard Business Review, 61*(3), 92–102.
Lucas, R. E., Jr. (1988). On the mechanics of economic development. *Journal of Monetary Economics, 22*(1), 3–42.
Malmberg, A., & Maskell, P. (1997). Towards an explanation of industry agglomeration and regional specialization. *European Planning Studies, 5*, 25–41.
McCann, B., & Folta, T. (2008). Location matters: Where we have been and where we might go in agglomeration research. *Journal of Management, 34*(3), 532–565.
Moon, H. C., Rugman, A., & Verbeke, A. (1995). The generalised double diamond approach to international competitiveness. In A. M. Rugman, J. van den Broeck, & A. Verbeke (Eds.), *Global strategic management (Vol. 5—beyond the diamond)*. London, UK: JAI Press.
Moon, H. C., Rugman, A., & Verbeke, A. (1998). A generalised double diamond approach to the global competitiveness of Korea and Singapore. *International Business Review, 7*(2), 135–150.
Neary, J. P. (2001). Of hype and hyperbolas: Introducing the new economic geography. *Journal of Economic Literature, 39*(2), 536–561.
Ottaviano, G., & Puga, D. (1998). Agglomeration in the global economy: A survey of the 'New Economic Geography'. *The World Economy, 21*(6), 707–731.

Ottaviano, G. I. P., & Thisse, J.-F. (2003). *Agglomeration and economic geography* (CEPR Discussion Paper No. 3838).

Pe'er, A., Vertinsky, I., & King, A. (2008). Who enters, where and why? The influence of capabilities and research endowments on the location choices of de novo enterprises. *Strategic Organization, 6*(2), 119–149.

Porter, M. E. (1990a). *The competitive advantage of nations*. New York: Free Press Macmillan.

Porter, M. E. (1990b). The competitive advantage of nations. *Harvard Business Review, 68*(2), 73–93.

Puga, D. (2002). European regional policies in light of recent location theories. *Journal of Economic Geography, 2*(4), 373–406.

Rugman, A., & D'Cruz, J. (1993). The 'double diamond' model of international competitiveness: The Canadian experience. *Management International Review, 33*(2), 17–40.

Saxenian, A. (1994). *Regional advantage: Culture and competition in Silicon Valley and Route 128*. Cambridge, MA: Harvard University Press.

Taylor, P. J., & Hoyler, M. (2000). The spatial order of European cities under conditions of contemporary globalisation. *Tijdschrift voor Economische en Sociale Geografie, 91*(2), 176–189.

Therborn, G. (1995). *European modernity and beyond. The trajectory of European societies 1945–2000*. London: Sage.

Thisse, J.-P. (2000). Agglomeration and regional imbalance: Why? And is it bad? *EIB Papers, 5*(2), 47–67.

Van Den Bulcke, D., Verbeke, A., & Yuan, W. (2009). *Handbook on small nations in the global economy open economy*. Cheltenham, UK: Edward Elgar.

4

Integrated Ports Clusters and Competitive Advantage in an Extended Resource Pool for the Antwerp Seaport

Elvira Haezendonck and Mychal Langenus

1 Introduction

Ports currently face an environment characterized by increased scale of carriers and vessel sizes, stakeholder opposition to port expansion, and heavy regulation. Therefore, ports are preparing strategic responses. A possible response could entail the development of strategic partnerships, or any form of collaboration, which could allow them to obtain one or more competitive advantages through more or alternative combinations of unique resources. This assumes of course that the specific type of collaboration does not lead to such a (low) level of competition, conflicting with antitrust regulation (Suárez-Alemán et al. 2017).

Two types of collaboration exist: vertical and horizontal collaboration. The former refers to collaboration along the supply chain or in

This chapter originally appeared as an article published in Maritime Policy and Management 45, online 09 May 2018. It is available https://doi.org/10.1080/03088839.2018.1471535.

E. Haezendonck (✉) · M. Langenus
Department of Business, Vrije Universiteit Brussel (VUB), Brussels, Belgium
e-mail: elvira.haezendonck@vub.be

E. Haezendonck and A. Verbeke (eds.), *Sustainable Port Clusters and Economic Development*, Palgrave Studies in Maritime Economics,
https://doi.org/10.1007/978-3-319-96658-8_4

the case of ports logistics chain, and which could also be termed "coordination." The latter refers, alternatively, to collaboration along a port range or between (competing) ports, also termed "cooperation" or "co-opetition" (Song 2003; Brooks et al. 2009). In this paper, we focus on port coordination and analyze its potential impact on creating more or new competitive advantages for the integrated port. Ports engage in coordination efforts, as they need to have a competitive advantage in contestable hinterlands (De Langen 2008). In fact, ports compete to a large extent by the efficiency and effectiveness of their hinterland networks (Robinson 2002; Notteboom and Rodrigue 2005). We divided the geographical scope of a port's coordinated or integrated network into respectively, from near to remote, three extents: proximate inland terminals, dry ports, and inland navigation terminals or hubs. A landlord port authority, although it has limited influence, can introduce various coordination mechanisms to influence the conditions under which hinterland transport networks work (Van der Horst and De Langen 2008; De Langen 2008). As put forward by Brooks et al. (2009: 40) research on port collaboration should look on "*what makes for successful cooperative activities.*" In addition, it is also interesting to look at cases where no substantial positive result occurs from collaborative efforts. In fact, ports may well enter into specific forms of collaboration without contemplating if such efforts will indeed result in positive outcomes.

We take an extended resource-based view perspective (McEvily and Zaheer 1999; Lavie 2006) to study the competitive advantages of an integrated port cluster. We apply the framework on the case of the port of Antwerp. The contributions of the study are twofold: first, the present study aims to determine empirically, based on an extended version of Porter's (1990) "diamond" framework, and on new data, the determinants of the competitive advantage of the Antwerp port cluster as compared to its rivals. Second, we compare the sources of competitive advantage found in the original value chain of ports based on the competitiveness matrix of Haezendonck et al. (2000) with the more relevant matrix today, given the integration of the port into its hinterland, and which is applied in this paper. Based on the vertical collaboration focus, we will analyze what could, or should drive port collaboration, and how an extension of a port's vertical boundaries actually impacts its competitiveness.

The structure of the study is as follows: in Sect. 2 we discuss the literature regarding competitive advantages of ports and the extension toward the hinterland. After that, Sect. 3 focuses on the adopted methodology. Results are provided in Sect. 4 and discussed in Sect. 5, before offering conclusions and policy recommendations in Sect. 6. Section 7 finally entails the limitations and recommendations for future research of the study.

2 Literature Review

2.1 Competitive Advantages of Ports

The resource-based view (RBV) theory defines that competitive advantages can be created if a firm is successful in the creation of a strategy that is based on resources that are difficult to be duplicated by a competitor (Barney 1991; Wernerfelt 1984). Such resources can be "*assets, capabilities, organizational processes, firm attributes, information, knowledge,* etc. *controlled by a firm*" (Barney 1991: 101). In order to be a potential source of competitive advantage, an underlying resource bundle must be rare, valuable, inimitable, and non-substitutable. Only if a unique bundle of resources is formed, perceived as valuable by customers and consciously deployed in a focal firm's strategy, can it be regarded as a competitive advantage. However, we must also note that once a competitive advantage has been attained, its sustainability in the longer run is not guaranteed (Barney 1991: 103).

Although various valid and complementary models exist to analyze competition and competitiveness of ports, such as a game-theoretical approach (applied by e.g., Anderson et al. 2008), ports co-option (e.g., Heaver et al. 2001; Song 2003), multicriteria analysis (e.g., Teng et al. 2004), and review studies leading to modeling frameworks for port competition have been conducted (e.g., Wan et al. 2018), the resource-based view has, for almost two decades now, proven its relevance and impact in (trans)port studies. Haezendonck et al. (2000) were the first to empirically analyze the competitive advantages of a seaport through the development and analysis of a matrix, by which they identified the port of Antwerp's competitiveness determinants. The matrix had on the horizontal axis the functional activities of the port from a logistics chain perspective (Cooper 1994), and on the vertical axis the resources as derived from the extended "diamond" framework of Porter. The extended "diamond" framework incorporates "government" as a fifth key element next to the four original elements of the diamond framework, which are: factor conditions, demand conditions, related and supporting industries and firm strategy, structure and rivalry (Porter 1990).

Later, Gordon et al. (2005) have applied the resource-based view to study the competitive advantage of the Port of Singapore (PSA) and Acosta et al. (2007) have analyzed the competitiveness of the Algeciras port using the extended diamond of Porter. Besides the interesting port-related findings, Gordon et al. (2005) propose that managers should, in their pursuit of attaining a superior yet sustainable competitive edge, not only consider the resources internal to the organization but also identify external resources, and furthermore develop internal resources that can build on those external resources, which relate to the earlier idea of "dynamic capabilities" developed by Teece et al. (1997). Through a continuous interaction of both types of resources, a competitive advantage could be sustained for a firm. Acosta et al. (2007) included all the institutions and companies involved in the containerization process, but those were not explicitly integrated in the port cluster from the port authority's perspective.

Interestingly in this context, McEvily and Zaheer (1999) put forward that the resource-based view can be extended to the network level or a cluster of organizations. A cluster can be defined as "geographic concentrations of interconnected companies, specialized suppliers, service providers, firms in related industries, and associated institutions (e.g. universities, standards agencies, trade associations) in a particular field that compete but also cooperate" (Porter 2000: 15). Network resources are then those resources, which are external to the focal firm but are embedded in the network, and offer strategic opportunities to influence the value of the focal firm (Lavie 2006). In line with Lavie (2006), Wassmer and Dussauge (2011), and Jans (2016), in combination with the previously stated findings of Teece et al. (1997), and Gordon et al. (2005), we follow the idea that the cluster environment offers the focal organisation an environment where network resources can be combined with the non-shared resources of the firm in a unique way, offering potential for new competitive advantages. In this way, performance heterogeneity can still exist, and in optimal cases a cluster firm would have superior performance relative to a non-cluster firm (Jans 2016).

2.2 Port Collaborative Network as Extended Resource Base

In general, inter-organizational alliances have risen in popularity since the 80s (Gulati 1998; Gulati et al. 2000; Hagedoorn 1993, 1995; Lavie 2006). Collaborative agreements can take many forms with the inter-organizational dependence, varying from negligible, e.g., in start-up assistance agreements or technical training, to high, e.g., co-production of goods or services or technology or equity joint ventures (Contractor and Lorange 1988; Song 2003). Two more general types of collaboration occur in the ports industry: vertical and horizontal collaboration. The former type refers to collaboration along the supply chain. This type of collaboration is also referred to as "coordination." The latter type refers, alternatively, to collaboration along a port range or between ports, also termed "cooperation" or "co-opetition" (Song 2003; Brooks et al. 2009). The World Bank, which commissioned a study in 2007 (The World Bank 2007) concerning inter-port cooperation, believes that neighboring ports can boost their competitiveness by working together and by innovating, and thus create additional salient sources of competitive advantage. Furthermore, Chiang and Hwang (2009) advocate that ports in the same region should cooperate and integrate to enhance competitiveness. Despite such reasoning, ports located in the same range usually compete fiercely for cargo and to maintain complete or partial control over customers, market share, and hinterlands (Marlow and Paixao 2001; Cahoon et al. 2013). The tendency of port authorities, located in the same geographical region, to compete rather than cooperate, has been earlier described by Wang and Slack (2004) and in the context of container port efficiency by Yap and Lam (2004). Shipping lines and operators, whose combined presence and market share in multiple ports gives them more power, have gained this power through consolidation and alliances. Their resulting, growing scale and importance to the port, may limit, in turn, the power and influence of the different port authorities downstream the port's value chain. Ports may respond to increase their power through for example mergers, more influence on its logistics chain, or any form of collaboration which results in a growing port influence, as suggested by Carbone and De Martino (2003) and Song and Panayides (2008). However, little is known today on the empirical outcome of port integration, expansion, or collaborative partnerships, in terms of increased competitiveness or measurable efficiency gains. Very recently, Cui (2017) found that port scale expansion does not necessarily lead to environmental gains, and Xing et al. (2018) revealed that port integration may well lead to a reduction of social welfare and consumer surplus. Those are at least two empirical studies which demonstrate that as regards port collaboration, not all that glitters is gold.

In this paper, we focus on vertical collaboration or port coordination whereby a port authority formally engages into activities which were previously under full responsibility or ownership of organizations other than the port authority. Ports compete to a large extent by the efficiency and effectiveness of their hinterland networks (Robinson 2002; Notteboom and Rodrigue 2005). Hence, ports engage in coordination efforts, as they need to have a competitive advantage incontestable hinterlands (De Langen 2008). The geographical scope of a port's integrated network can be divided into respectively, from near to remote, three extents: proximate inland terminals, dry ports, and inland navigation terminals, or hubs. We have chosen this distinction in order for our results to be related to either remote or more distant collaborative efforts, of which some distinct cases do exist today for some European hubs, for example HAROPA, Antwerp port's collaborative agreement with the port of Liège, Rotterdam's willingness to take a large stake in Duisburg port, Thus, although a port authority has a limited domain of influence—under the most common form of a landlord port authority—a port authority can introduce different types of coordination mechanisms to impact the conditions under which hinterland transport networks work (Van der Horst and De Langen 2008;

De Langen 2008; Rodrigue and Notteboom 2009). However (trans) port and maritime literature has not offered many insights in the vertical type of collaboration, and more specifically into which advantages or disadvantages this may or may not bring for a focal organization such as a port authority or cluster manager (e.g., De Martino et al. 2013; Hoshino 2010).

2.3 Hinterland Extension: The Port Network

Many authors have expressed the salience of the port network as a research unit to analyze regional container hub rivalry (Hayut 1981; Slack 1985; van der Horst and van der Lugt 2011). Ports in the same range compete for traffic volumes from and to shippers in their hinterland. Rodrigue (2010) identified hinterland connections as a key factor in port competitiveness. Good connections to the hinterland have become more relevant in the competition among container seaports, as ports are no longer considered as single actors, but as key parts of the logistics chain. With the optimization of logistics and inland transport networks, more shippers in an extending hinterland could potentially be reached via seaports. How well a seaport succeeds in efficiently reaching this extended hinterland, through, for example, participations in inland terminals, may as such co-determine its competitiveness. It may enable inland corridor formation, allowing load centers to access formerly captive hinterlands of other ports. With increasingly captive hinterlands, inter-port competition has increased as well. This inter-port competition, in combination with the complexity of hinterland logistics, requires ports to be more proactive in their hinterland strategies. Hinterland connections have thus become an essential part of the ports' distinct value propositions (Bergqvist 2012). Especially, since inland transport nodes are becoming more and more essential due to the saturation of terminal storage capacity and the shipping liners adoption of hub-and-spoke distribution strategies (Ducruet and Notteboom 2012).

Rodrigue et al. (2009) underline the growing inter-port hinterland competition and state that the development of land transport has allowed ports and their container terminals to extend their hinterlands to reach captive markets from other ports of their region. Hence, ports can be seen as elements in a value-driven chain, whereby the port captures value for itself and for the chain it is a part of (Robinson 2002). This is already argued by Notteboom and Winkelmans (2001), who state that seaports and shipping lines vertically integrate to further control hinterland transport. Wilmsmeier et al. (2011) add to this that port authorities have a role in this, and need to be active in extending or maintaining their hinterland. The more dominant role of the ports in the hinterland is also in evidence offered by Haralambides and Gujar (2011), who argue that the overall supply chain can benefit from an extension of the sea-terminal connection into the hinterland. This extension has multiple positive effects, e.g., overall benefits in terms of the logistics chain's performance, modal shift opportunities, and regional development effects.

Given the expected positive influence of an integrated hinterland for seaports to compete, we decided to analyze this for three distance related levels of integration: proximate inland terminals, dry ports, and inland navigation terminals, or hubs. The first level is based on the extended gate concept. Veenstra et al. (2012) consider new responsibilities in addition to being a "stocking point"; they propose supply chain and transportation network integration by extending the sea-terminal gate into the hinterland, the extended gate. They argue that extended gates, when implemented correctly, can generate substantial benefits in terms of modal shift, logistics performance, and regional development, and therefore contribute to the competitiveness of seaports. The second level can be supported by Notteboom and Winkelmans (2004) and Cullinane et al. (2012), who state that also dry ports play an important role in the competitiveness of seaports. According to these authors, to remain valid, container terminals are obliged to constantly reassess their customers, to reconfigure competitive concepts like the hinterland, foreland, and captive markets, and to extend their role in the supply chain through the inland integration of port services. Cheung et al. (2003) dig deeper into the possible advantages of advancing further into the hinterland through inland hubs: this might often be attractive for shippers to outsource value-adding services such as packaging and sequencing to logistics service providers at strategically placed nodes.

The third level finds support in Van den Berg and De Langen (2011) and Verhoeven (2009), who claim that inland terminals play a crucial role in the competitive position of the port in the hinterland, as ports have become dependent on intermodal transport networks to maintain or extend their competitive position.

In sum, the competitiveness of a port today seems to heavily depend upon the network in which it operates. Instead of restricted to the functions within the seaport area itself, an extension of the logistics chain is part of the new business model of port authorities. Hence, the basic assumption for this paper is that the extended resource base of today's integrated ports would lead to more opportunities for creating competitive advantages for ports.

We build on the competitiveness-matrix developed by Haezendonck et al. (2000), where functional activities performed within the port from a logistics chain perspective (Cooper 1994) were combined in a matrix with the resources required to perform those activities, as suggested by the extended diamond framework of competitive advantage (Porter 1990). In fact, we have added the port network within the logistics chain perspective, being the elements on the horizontal axis of the matrix. This network dimension is added on the right in the matrix, see Fig. 1, with the green colored columns, adding potential determinants to the original competitiveness matrix (Haezendonck et al. 2000), which leads to a new, extended competitiveness matrix as shown in Fig. 1.

In Fig. 1, the columns under *port network* stretch the port value chain further into the hinterland, and consists based on the above of the three sub-columns: proximate inland terminals, dry ports, and inland navigation terminals/hubs. These columns detail port value creating activities gradually located more inland than the original activities considered based on port logistic chain activities as considered by Haezendonck et al. (2000) in their competitiveness matrix using Button's (1993) value activities for ports. The proximate inland terminal refers to the area just outside the port area, and the dry port refers to inland located intermodal terminals, which connect the port with the hinterland and might be a potential base of extended activity of the port itself, defined by UNCTAD (1982), i.e., as a place inland that fulfills

Diamond determinants	Logistics chain	Maritime access		Activities port sector						Hinterland transport			Port network		
		Activities maritime accessibility -ACCESS	Shipping -SHIP	Transshipment -LOAD	Warehousing -WARE	Value added logistics -VAL	Manufacturing -MANU	Activities by shipping agents, forwarders -EXP	Distribution activities within cluster -DISTR	Road -ROAD	Rail -RAIL	Inland navigation -INAV	Proximate inland terminals -PROX	Dry ports -DRY	Inland navigation terminals/hubs -INTER
Factor conditions	infrastructure INFR-	INFR-ACCES	INFR-SHIP	INFR-LOAD	INFR-WARE	INFR-VAL	INFR-MANU	INFR-EXP	INFR-DISTR	INFR-ROAD	INFR-RAIL	INFR-INAV	INFR-PROX	INFR-DRY	INFR-INTER
	superstructure SUP-	SUP-ACCESS	SUP-SHIP	SUP-LOAD	SUP-WARE	SUP-VAL	SUP-MANU	SUP-EXP	SUP-DISTR	SUP-ROAD	SUP-RAIL	SUP-INAV	SUP-PROX	SUP-DRY	SUP-INTER
	Human capital LAB-	LAB-ACCESS	LAB-SHIP	LAB-LOAD	LAB-WARE	LAB-VAL	LAB-MANU	LAB-EXP	LAB-DISTR	LAB-ROAD	LAB-RAIL	LAB-INAV	LAB-PROX	LAB-DRY	LAB-INTER
	Logistical technology and communication systems LOG-	LOG-ACCESS	LOG-SHIP	LOG-LOAD	LOG-WARE	LOG-VAL	LOG-MANU	LAG-EXP	LOG-DISTR	LOG-ROAD	LOG-RAIL	LOG-INAV	LOG-PROX	LOG-DRY	LOG-INTER
Firm strategy, structure and rivalry	Intra-cluster competition ICO-	ICO-ACCESS	ICO-SHIP	ICO-LOAD	ICO-WARE	ICO-VAL	ICO-MANU	ICO-EXP	ICO-DISTR	ICO-ROAD	ICO-RAIL	ICO-INAV	ICO-PROX	ICO-DRY	ICO-INTER
	Inter-cluster competition ECO-	ECO-ACCESS	ECO-SHIP	ECO-LOAD	ECO-WARE	ECO-VAL	ECO-MANU	ECO-EXP	ECO-DISTR	ECO-ROAD	ECO-RAIL	ECO-INAV	ECO-PROX	ECO-DRY	ECO-INTER
	Internal co-operation ICOOP-	ICOOP-ACCESS	ICOOP-SHIP	ICOOP-LOAD	ICOOP-WARE	ICOOP-VAL	ICOOP-MANU	ICOOP-EXP	ICOOP-DISTR	ICOOP-ROAD	ICOOP-RAIL	ICOOP-INA	ICOOP-PROX	ICOOP-DRY	ICOOP-INTER
	External co-operation ECOOP-	ECOOP-ACCESS	ECOOP-SHIP	ECOOP-LOAD	ECOOP-WARE	ECOOP-VAL	ECOOP-MANU	ECOOP-EXP	ECOOP-DISTR	ECOOP-ROAD	ECOOP-RAIL	ECOOP-INA	ECOOP-PROX	ECOOP-DRY	ECOOP-INTER
Demand conditions	Client relationships in cluster ICLI-	ICLI-ACCESS	ICLI-SHIP	ICLI-LOAD	ICLI-WARE	ICLI-VAL	ICLI-MANU	ICLI-EXP	ICLI-DISTR	ICLI-ROAD	ICLI-RAIL	ICLI-INAV	ICLI-PROX	ICLI-DRY	ICLI-INTER
	Client relationships outside cluster ECLI-	ECLI-ACCESS	ECLI-SHIP	ECLI-LOAD	ECLI-WARE	ECLI-VAL	ECLI-MANU	ECLI-EXP	ECLI-DISTR	ECLI-ROAD	ECLI-RAIL	ECLI-INAV	ECLI-PROX	ECLI-DRY	ECLI-INTER
Government	Government intervention (port authority) GOLOC-	GOLOC-ACCESS	GOLOC-SHIP	GOLOC-LOAD	GOLOC-WARE	GOLOC-VAL	GOLOC-MANU	GOLOC-EXP	GOLOC-DISTR	GOLOC-ROAD	GOLOC-RAIL	GOLOC-INA	GOLOC-PROX	GOLOC-DRY	GOLOC-INTER
	Government intervention (regional) GOREG-	GOREC-ACCESS	GOREC-SHIP	GOREC-LOAD	GOREC-WARE	GOREC-VAL	GOREC-MANU	GOREC-EXP	GOREC-DISTR	GOREC-ROAD	GOREC-RAIL	GOREC-INA	GOREG-PROX	GOREG-DRY	GOREG-INTER
	Government intervention (national, supranational) GONAT-	GONAT-ACCESS	GONAT-SHIP	GONAT-LOAD	GONAT-WARE	GONAT-VAL	GONAT-MANU	GONAT-EXP	GONAT-DISTR	GONAT-ROAD	GONAT-RAIL	GONAT-INA	GONAT-PROX	GONAT-DRY	GONAT-INTER
Related and supporting industries	Port supporting services (bank, insurance) SERV-	SERV-ACCESS	SERV-SHIP	SERV-LOAD	SERV-WARE	SERV-VAL	SERV-MANU	SERV-EXP	SERV-DISTR	SERV-ROAD	SERV-RAIL	SERV-INAV	SERV-PROX	SERV-DRY	SERV-INTER

Fig. 1 New competitiveness matrix for the port of Antwerp (*Source* Authors, extended based on Haezendonck et al. [2000])

original port functions. The inland navigation terminals/hubs refer to the existence of a port cluster from inland terminals and inland ports with whom the port is in a structural relationship, for example, by taking shares in these terminals or being a member of their board. The advantages of the implementation of the dry port concept may come from decreasing port congestion, alleviating pressure on storage space, reducing handling operations and time spent in ports, and lowering transaction costs to shippers. This dry port function has been described by Roso et al. (2009): inland intermodal terminals, directly connected to a seaport by rail, which enables activities to be transferred from the seaport to a more inland located trimodal logistic location to relieve congestion and achieve other benefits (e.g., potential of modal split, multimodal platform).

3 Empirical Analysis of Competitiveness Determinants of the Integrated Antwerp Seaport Cluster

In this section, we explain how we collected and analyzed our data for the extended competitiveness matrix. We introduce the sample, survey method, and elaborate on data analysis before we present the results in Sect. 4.

3.1 Sample and Method

By means of a questionnaire, including the extended competitiveness matrix, used as a basis for interviewing 59 C-level managers from June 2013 until December 2013, the competitive advantages and disadvantages of the port cluster of Antwerp, vis-à-vis the main competitors for containers and conventional cargo in the Hamburg-Le Havre range ports, were determined. We identified all potential expert-participants by researching which organizations were involved in the core business of the extended port cluster and in the container traffic segment in particular. The selected experts were mostly responsible for the strategic/planning department of the ports main actors (N, N-1, and N-2 management levels), i.e., terminal operators, shipping companies, agents, forwarders, experts and also some key industrial actors in the port area, mainly petrochemical companies in the Antwerp seaport.

3.2 Survey Method

The first part of the questionnaire contained general questions, related to the size and scope of the company active in the Antwerp port and its traffic specialization. The second and main part of the interview was based on the port's "extended competitiveness-matrix" (see Fig. 1). The third part of the questionnaire contained open-ended questions, which allowed for better understanding and interpreting of the different scores of the competitiveness matrix. The survey was complemented with a separate, detailed list of all matrix variables and their definition, in order to make clear what is meant by each variable. In practice, the respondents had this sheet next to the competitiveness matrix when providing their answers. All interviews took place at the office of the expert-participants. Two experiences researchers, of which one has been responsible for several similar surveys in the past 2 decades, personally carried out all interviews and noted down themselves the answers provided by the respondents. This allowed for a structured process, with structured criteria.

Each variable (cell) in the extended competitiveness matrix represents the combination of an individual activity (in columns, 14 in total) with a selected resource (in rows, 14 in total), with its name based on the abbreviation of the respective resource and activity in the port cluster (Fig. 1). For example, the variable that combines the infrastructure (INFR-) that is necessary for maritime accessibility (-ACCES) is named "INFRACCES." In line with the more limited analysis of port competitiveness determinants in 1998 (Haezendonck et al. 2000), all respondents were asked to provide a discrete score (−2 to +2 on a five-point Likert-scale) for all variables in the matrix in terms of each variable's perceived negative or positive impact on the competitiveness of the port of Antwerp compared to its main rivals in the Hamburg—Le Havre range. The neutral score 0 was given for those variables considered neither an advantage, nor a disadvantage for the port cluster. Each variable can be viewed as a single source of co-determinant of a seaport cluster's competitiveness, on which competitive advantages or disadvantages may be built.

3.3 Descriptive Statistics and Data Analysis

For each respondent included in the survey, we obtained a completed extended competitiveness matrix, with scores for 196 variables. The following steps were taken to raise the validity of the interviews: first, interviews were conducted by the same team of two researchers; second, each identified stakeholder group (shipping liners, operators, agencies, and experts) had more than 15 respondents, and industrial actors were sufficiently represented as well. For example, experts from all major shipping companies within the container alliances operating at the data collection period, see Table 1, and operating in the port of Antwerp, were surveyed.

Table 1 Major alliances and their members in 2015

2 M	28.3%	CKYHE	17.1%	G6	18.4%	Ocean Three	14.6%
Maersk	15.1%	COSCO	4.3%	APL	2.9%	CMA CGM	8.9%
MSC	13.2%	"K" Line	2.0%	Hapag-Lloyd	5.0%	CSCL	3.6%
		Yang Ming	2.4%	HMM	1.9%	UASC	2.1%
		Hanjin	3.3%	MOL	3.2%		
		Evergreen	5.1%	NYK Line	2.5%		
				OOCL	2.9%		

The percentages represent the share of the shipping line as a percentage of the world fleet
Source Based on Alphaliner top 100. Retrieved from http://www.alphaliner.com/top100/, last consulted on July 6th 2015

However, prior to further analysis, bias correction was necessary for multiple reasons: first, to avoid possible bias caused by the potentiality of the results of the study being used for political lobbying (Haezendonck et al. 2011); second, as with the earlier study (Haezendonck et al. 2000) a number of respondents systematically gave more extreme answers, whereas others were more moderate; this was probably due to variations in personality or attitudes of the respondents rather than a reflection of factual differences in the parameters underlying the competitiveness of the port of Antwerp. To adjust for this, *z*-scores were computed per respondent by centering on the average and scaling by the standard deviation of the whole respondent sample.

Based on the survey data collected in this average competitiveness *z*-matrix, linear regression analysis was performed using IBM SPSS statistics version 22.0, to reveal which activities (variables in columns) and resources (variables in rows) receive a positive or negative value. The regression model attempts to explain the scores in the average *z*-matrix by means of two categorical variables, namely the row and column indices. We encoded these categorical variables by binary dummy variables. The regression model was tested for multicollinearity (expressed as the variance inflation factor—VIF) and the standardized residuals, computed by this regression model for each cell of the matrix, were normally distributed. These residuals represent the difference between the real value of the *z*-score of each variable in the matrix and the estimated/fitted value of the *z*-score as predicted by the linear regression model. If the residuals are roughly normally distributed, around 95% of them should lie between the cut-off values of −2.5 and 2.5. Cells of the matrix that corresponded with a standard residual value higher than 2.5 or lower than −2.5 were considered as basic sources of competitive advantages or disadvantages, respectively.

Additionally, we also applied factor analysis to understand how the individual high or low-scoring variables (the activities and resources of the extended competitiveness matrix) interact with each other. Hence, a potential relation between activities, see Table 2, or resources, see Table 3, could be detected, and we are able to screen for underlying dimensions in our data set or in other words for the existence of

Table 2 Factor analysis on perceived value of the activities (2013)

	Factor	
	1	2
ACCESS	.706	.180
SHIP	.607	.135
LOAD	.784	.250
WARE	.695	.166
VAL	.709	.251
MANU	.481	.380
EXP	.821	.290
DISTR	.639	.416
ROAD	.361	.617
RAIL	.283	.552
INAV	.267	.701
PROX	.266	.779
DRY	.126	.950
INTER	.191	.882

Source Results of the factor analysis (maximum likelihood), with Varimax rotation and Kaiser normalization of the value of the activities. The extracted factors account for a cumulative explained variance of 64.6%

Table 3 Factor analysis on the perceived value of the resources (2013)

	Factor			
	1	2	3	4
INFR	.742		.147	−.234
SUP	.655	.420	.277	−.228
LAB	.680	.139		.130
LOG	.105	.216		−.584
ICO	.775		.270	
ECO	.403			.165
ICOOP	.354	.185		.481
ECOOP	.428	.355	.200	.192
ICLI		.755		−.129
ECLI	.140	.561		.119
GOLOC	.240		.954	.159
GOREG	.333		.300	.315
GONAT		.143	.522	−.155
SERV		.598	.178	−.173

Source Results of the factor analysis (maximum likelihood), with Varimax rotation and Kaiser normalization of value of the resources. The extracted factors account for a cumulative explained a bundling phase of resources. These underlying dimensions are called factors.

To perform factor analysis on our dataset, the average score for the activity/resource for each respondent was calculated. For example, the average score for INFR in combination with all activities was calculated for each respondent. Consequently, this average score for INFR from each respondent was standardized by centering on the average and scaling by the standard deviation of the average score for INFR for all 59 respondents. This standardization made it easy to check for the correlations between all the different activities/resources. On this dataset, factor analysis (maximum likelihood) with Varimax rotation and Kaiser normalization as the rotation method was applied.

4 Results

4.1 Results from the Extended Competitive Data Analysis

When including the added port network elements in columns (in short: DRY, PROX, INTER) as determinants in the second regression analysis (explained variance of 61.8%, with a VIF value of 1.857) in order to explore the new competitive position of the port of Antwerp, we observe a rather neutral impact for these three resources, as shown in Fig. 2 (in full black lines) and Fig. 3 (in full black dots). In other words, no significant positive or negative perceived value resulted from these added elements.

Based on the extended competitiveness-matrix results, linear regression analysis was applied as described above. From this analysis, we obtained the main effect of each activity (row) and resource (column) of the matrix. In Fig. 2, these are plotted with the main effects of the resources on the horizontal axis and the main effects of the activities on the vertical axis. The relative position of these values is a measure of the overall perceived value of both activities (columns) and resources (rows). We can clearly observe two outliers on the horizontal axis, RAIL (negative) and WARE (positive), in relation to the other variables.

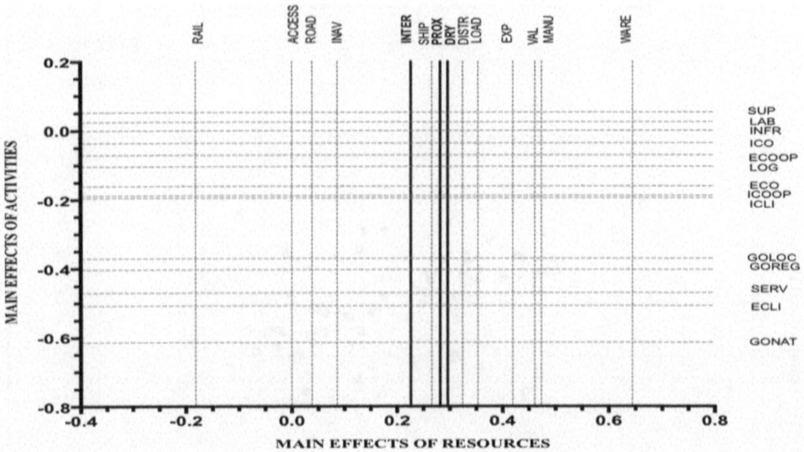

Fig. 2 Plot of the main effects of the activities and the resources (*The dotted lines in grey represent the variables of the classic competitiveness matrix; the full lines in black represent the variables of the added port network components (i.e., PROX, INTER, DRY). Source* Based on the results of regression analysis on the extended competitiveness matrix in SPSS)

From the main effects of the resources, we can observe an overall somewhat negative result.

To visualize the detected interactions, we plotted the standardized residuals (Fig. 3). These residuals represent the difference between the real value of the *z*-score of each variable in the matrix and the estimated/fitted value of the *z*-score as predicted by the linear regression model. If the residuals are roughly normally distributed, around 95% of them should lie between the cut-off values of −2.5 and 2.5, which are presented as horizontal lines. Values lying far above or below these boundaries are outliers, referring to positive or negative interactions. In this figure, INFRWARE and SUPWARE are both identified as positive outliers, whereas INFRACCES appears to be a negative outlier.

Figure 4 is a combination of Figs. 2 and 3, i.e., the plot of the main effects of the activities (rows) and resources (columns) and the plot of the standardized residuals versus the fitted *z*-scores. In this three-dimensional plot, the standardized residuals are plotted for each activity and corresponding resource, sorted by main effect, respectively.

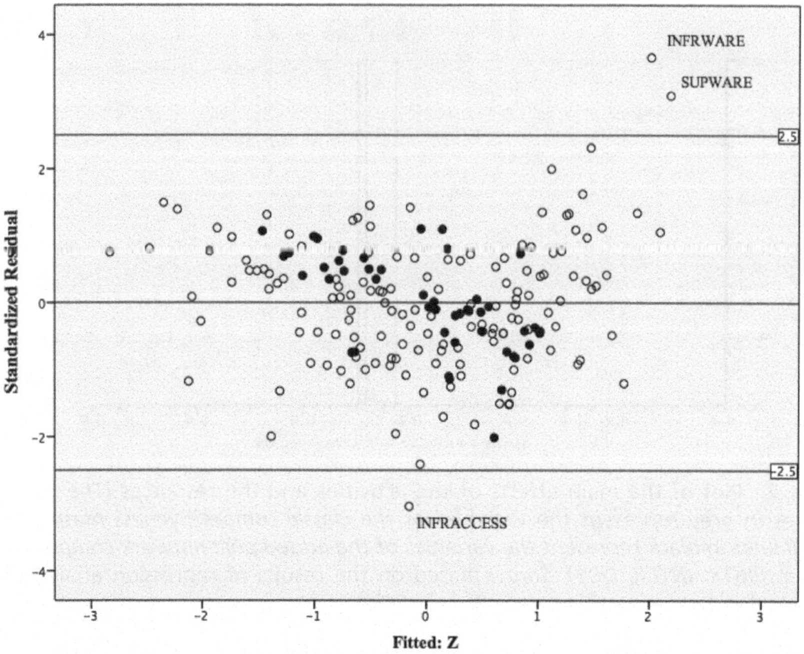

Fig. 3 Plot of the standardized residuals versus the fitted *z*-scores (The labeled points are the cells with the largest interaction. *The white dots represent the variables of the classic competitiveness matrix, the black dots represent the variables of the added port network elements (i.e., PROX, INTER, DRY). Source* Based on the results of regression analysis on the extended competitiveness matrix in SPSS)

The peaks and valleys in this plot correspond with the respectively positive and negative outliers found in Fig. 3.

Based on Figs. 3 and 4, we can observe important positive interactions between "infrastructure" and "warehousing" on the one hand, and "superstructure" and "warehousing" on the other (INFRWARE and SUPWARE).

Negative interactions (INFRACCES) can be observed between "infrastructure" and "maritime access." Concerning the results of the factor analyses on the perceptions of respondents, to define a set of crucial factors underlying the competitiveness of the Antwerp port cluster, two underlying factors were identified for the activities (see Table 2), whereas four factors could be extracted for the resources (see Table 3).

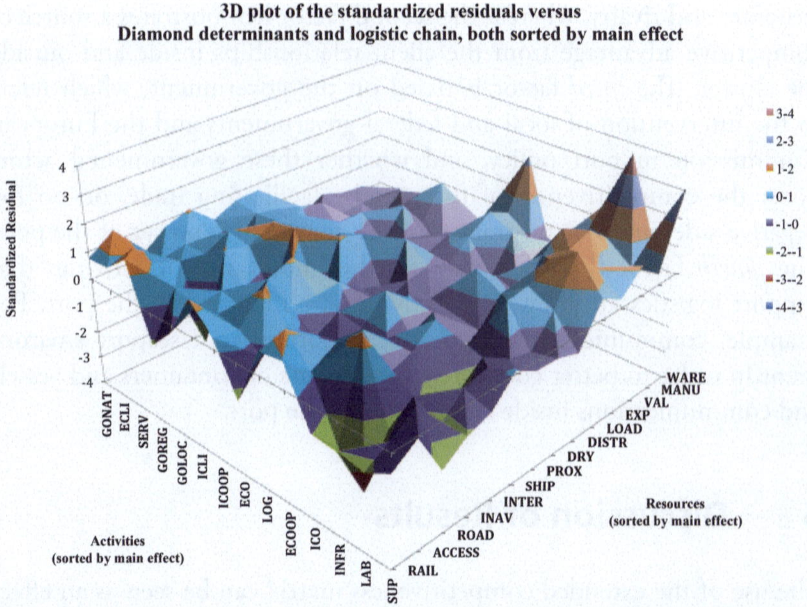

Fig. 4 Three-dimensional plot of the standardized residuals versus activity and resource, both sorted by main effect (*Source* Based on the results of regression analysis on the extended competitiveness matrix in SPSS)

For the activities, as represented in Table 2, factor one is determined primarily by activities in the port area (transshipment, warehousing activities, value added services, local industries, shipping agents and forwarding companies, and distribution activities in port) and factor two for the transporting activity to and from a port's hinterland. The *first* factor identified could therefore be viewed as "activities within the local port area itself." This means that the treatment of the ship, the moment it enters the port of Antwerp until it leaves the port of Antwerp, is still considered the Antwerp port's principal source of advantage vis-à-vis its rivals. The *second* factor is determined by the hinterland transport (inland navigation and road).

The factor analysis of the attributes of the port of Antwerp reveals four important factors, and the results hereof are shown in Table 3. The *first* factor is based on the factor conditions and firm strategy, structure and rivalry, whereas the second factor demonstrates a source of competitive advantage from the client relationships inside and outside the cluster. The *third* factor is based on the government, which refers to the intervention of local and federal governments and the European Commission in port policy, and whether these governmental actors boost the competitiveness of the port by facilitating trade, or, on the negative side, impose constraints on the competitive power of the port. The *fourth* factor (log) demonstrates the importance of activities that support logistics and how such activities are managed in the port. For example, communication systems are important in a seaport environment in order to better coordinate movements of containers and vessels and communications inside and outside of the port.

5 Discussion of Results

The use of the extended competitiveness matrix can be seen as an effective benchmarking tool for today's capturing of strengths and weaknesses underlying a port cluster's competitiveness, in this case of the port of Antwerp in comparison with its main competitors. Based on Figs. 3 and 4, variables INFRWARE and SUPWARE scored significantly positive, indicating the quality, capacity, and the diversified portfolio of these warehouses, being very salient for attracting and retaining shipping lines.

A negative interaction for INFRACCES was observed, which is between "infrastructure" and "maritime access," mainly due to the remaining time loss for ships entering the port benchmarked with Antwerp's rivals. The deepening of the Scheldt is moreover a continuous and expensive process.

The respondents also explained that the productivity and flexibility of the labor pool was the main underlying reason for Antwerp's competitive edge.

In fact, and when comparing with the original results of Haezendonck et al. (2000), only the availability of warehouses is revealed as a new, unique strength which may underlie a competitive advantage of the port.

Most strikingly, we found no particular significant sources of competitive advantage of the port related to its recent integration efforts into the hinterland. We have found that the port cluster of Antwerp has indeed not acquired a significant competitive edge in the battle for the hinterland, at least not if integration was part of this strategy.

6 Conclusions and Policy Implications

In the recent context of increased power of shipping alliances, and reduced government support if no efficient scale is seemingly reached, ports strategically respond by integrating actively into their logistics chain. Various experts as well as papers in the academic literature suggest that this should allow ports to extend their valuable resources pool so that more sources of competitive advantages can be available to ports.

In this paper, we build on the extended resource-based view perspective (McEvily and Zaheer 1999; Lavie 2006), and we analyze the competitive advantages of the Antwerp port cluster, integrated into parts of its hinterland network area. In fact, the port undertakes collaborative actions in its direct to more distant hinterland by taking shares in terminals, building relationships through positions in boards of dry ports, etc., and aims to control, or at least tap into resources from these extended organizational borders after one or another form of integration. As observed before, such combination of internal and external, and/or non-shared and shared, resources can result in the creation of new, sustainable competitive advantages. Furthermore, ports are nowadays less competing as individual firms but more so as nodes in supply chains, which again compete with other supply chains. We therefore investigate if the extension in the port's network leads to additional sources of competitive advantages, vis-à-vis the competitive advantages obtained from within the originally more limited port area or strategically controlled by the authority. We would expect so, given that literature suggests that seaports should extend their view on resources beyond their own boundaries.

Our empirical analysis, based on an extended competitiveness matrix, and deploying a robust methodology as applied by Haezendonck et al. (2000), did however not prove that this port's integration strategy into its hinterland has been successful up until now and given the current scope of integration of the Antwerp seaport into its hinterland. It needs to be stressed that this research is exploratory in nature and somehow premature or at least in an early stage of integration and research development. We need more research efforts and cases for a discussion of precisely how the proposed findings and mechanisms might operate. Various relationships with a port's hinterland may need (more) time to develop and may also be very case dependent. That said, the results as shown in this paper point out that port integration into its hinterland, as a form of port collaboration, or a scale or scope extending strategy, does not automatically, nor immediately, lead to an increased competitiveness potential.

7 Limitations and Future Research

The results found in this analysis could be due to the case itself or to the specific level or nature of integration that the seaport has undertaken until the year of our data analysis. Other cases of integration of seaports that function as hubs around the globe, potentially with other governance structures, or activity scope, or other time frames—given that integration is a dynamic process which can vary over time—may provide additional interesting insights.

Further research could also focus on the (opportunistic) behavior of port authorities in exploiting future competitive advantages or developing dynamic capabilities. Additionally, it would be interesting to investigate how a particular port network evolves in the future, and if and how its competitiveness follows those dynamics.

Acknowledgements The authors would like to thank Prof. Dr. Alain Verbeke (Vrije Universiteit Brussel) for the provision of the financial support that allowed the data collection of this research, through the GOA project. For the statistical analyses included, the authors would like to thank Toon Valaert for his valuable contribution.

Funding: This work was supported by VUB, grant number GOA-75.

Annex 1: Interview Template: Determinants of Port Competitiveness

1. General identification

A. Company : ………………
B. Address : ………………
C. Phone : …/……………
D. Fax : …/……………
E. Company activity : ………………
F. Respondent : ………………
G. Function : ………………
H. Company indicators:

Year	Turnover	Cash Flow	Employment	Tonnage
	………	………	………	………
	………	………	………	………
	………	………	………	………

2. **Competitiveness of the port of Antwerp: competitiveness-matrix and open-ended questions**

Question 1: - most important traffic category: ……………………………………………………………………………

- most important origin/destination: ………………………………………………………………………

- Is that traffic * basic 'captive' traffic (location, etc)

  * advanced 'captive' traffic (EDI, distribution, ….)?

What is the port of reference for that traffic category? ………………………………………………………

Give a score from -2 to +2 on the elements in the Table. Compare the port of Antwerp to its 'port of reference' (benchmark)

Possible scores:

-2: very weak position of the port of Antwerp
-1: weak
0: neutral (not weak, not strong)
+1: strong
+2: very strong
9: no opinion (missing value)

Table: NEW COMPETITIVENESS MATRIX

1. Logist	MARITIME		ACTIVITIES						HINTERLAND			PORT NETWORK		
	Activities maritime accessibility	Shipping companies	Trans-shipment	Ware-housing	Logistical service	Local industries	Shipping agents and Forwarding companies	Distribution activities in port	Road	Rail	Inland navigation	Proximate inland terminals	Dry ports	Inland navigation terminals/hubs
Infrastructure														
Superstructure														
Human capital														
Logistic technology and communication systems (informatics, EDI,…)														
Intra-port competition														
Inter-port competition														

Internal co-operation														
External co-operation														
Client relationships in port														
Client relationships outside port														
Local government intervention (port authority)														
Regional government intervention (Flanders)														
(Supra)national Government intervention (Belgium, EC)														
Port supporting services (banking, insurance, etc)														

Question 2: **If you could give a +3, to which variable would you give it and why?** ....

If you could give a –3, to which variable would you give it and why?....................

Question 3: **What impact will the weak scores have on the competitive position of the Antwerp seaport in the future, given an unchanged government policy?**

....

Given your perceptions, which elements deserve priority in policy?

....

What needs to be done concretely?

....

Question 4: **Which opportunities and threats do you think will be influencing severely the Antwerp seaport's competitiveness as regards containers?**

....

Thank you for your kind co-operation

References

Acosta, M., Coronado, D., & Mar Cerban, M. (2007). Port competitiveness in container traffic from an internal point of view: The experience of the Port of Algeciras Bay. *Maritime Policy & Management, 34*(5), 501–520.

Anderson, C. M., Park, Y. A., Chang, Y. T., Yang, C. H., Lee, T. W., & Luo, M. (2008). A game-theoretic analysis of competition among container port hubs: The case of Busan and Shanghai. *Maritime Policy & Management, 35*(1), 5–26.

Barney, J. B. (1991). Firm resources and sustained competitive advantage. *Journal of Management, 17*(1), 99–120.

Bergqvist, R. (2012). Hinterland logistics and global supply chains. In D. W. Song & P. Panayides (Eds.), *Maritime logistics: A complete guide to effective shipping and port management*. London: Kogan Page.

Brooks, M., Mccalla, R., Pallis, A., & van der Lugt, L. (2009). Strategic cooperation in peripheral ports: The case of Atlantic Canada's ports. *Canadian Journal of Transportation, 4*(1), 29–42.

Button, K. J. (1993). *Transport economics* (2nd ed.). Cheltenham: Edward Elgar.

Cahoon, S., Pateman, H., & Chen, S. L. (2013). Regional port authorities: Leading players in innovation networks? *Journal of Transport Geography, 27,* 66–75.

Carbone, V., & De Martino, M. (2003). The changing role of ports in supply-chain management: An empirical analysis. *Maritime Policy & Management, 30*(4), 305–320.

Chiang, C. H., & Hwang, C. C. (2009). Competitiveness of container ports in a region with cooperation and integration. *Journal of the Society for Transportation and Traffic Studies, 1,* 77–91.

Cheung, R., Tong, J., & Slack, B. (2003). The transition from freight consolidation to logistics: The case of Hong Kong. *Journal of Transport Geography, 11,* 245–253.

Contractor, F., & Lorange, P. (1988). Why should firms co-operate?—The strategy and economics basis for co-operative ventures. In F. Contractor & P. Lorange (Eds.), *Co-operative strategies in international business* (pp. 3–30). New York: Lexington Books.

Cooper, M. C. (1994). *Logistics in the decade of the 1990s.* New York: The Free Press.

Cui, Q. (2017). Environmental efficiency measures for ports: An application of RAM-Tobit-RAM with undesirable outputs. *Maritime Policy & Management, 44*(5), 551–564.

Cullinane, K., Bergqvist, R., & Wilmsmeier, G. (2012). The dry port concept—Theory and practice. *Maritime Economics & Logistics, 14*(1), 1–13.

De Langen, P. W. (2008). *Ensuring hinterland access the role of port authorities.* OECD/ITF, Joint Transport Research Centre, Discussion Paper, 18p.

De Martino, M., Errichiello, L., Marasco, A., & Morvillo, A. (2013). Logistics innovation in seaports: An inter-organizational perspective. *Research in Transportation Business & Management, 8,* 123–133.

Ducruet, C., & Notteboom, T. (2012). Developing liner service networks in container shipping. In D. W. Song & P. Panayides (Eds.), *Maritime logistics: A complete guide to effective shipping and port management* (pp. 77–100). London: Kogan Page.

Gordon, J. R., Lee, P. M., & Lucas, H. C. (2005). A resource-based view of competitive advantage at the Port of Singapore. *The Journal of Strategic Information Systems, 14*(1), 69–86.

Gulati, R. (1998). Alliances and networks. *Strategic Management Journal, 19*, 293–317.

Gulati, R., Nohria, N., & Zaheer, A. (2000). Strategic networks. *Strategic Management Journal, 21*(Special Issue), 203–215.

Hagedoorn, J. (1993). Understanding the rationale of strategic technology partnering. *Strategic Management Journal, 14*, 371–385.

Hagedoorn, J. (1995). Strategic technology partnering during the 1980s: Trends, networks, and corporate patterns in non-core technologies. *Research Policy, 24*, 207–231.

Haezendonck, E., Pison, G., Rousseeuw, P., Struyf, A., & Verbeke, A. (2000). The competitive advantage of seaports. *International Journal of Maritime Economics, 2*(2), 69–82.

Haezendonck, E., van den Broeck, J., & Jans, T. (2011). Analysing the lobby-effect of port competitiveness' determinants: A stochastic frontier approach. *Journal of Productivity Analysis, 36*(2), 113–123.

Haralambides, H., & Gujar, G. (2011). The Indian dry ports sector, pricing policies and opportunities for public-private partnerships. *Research in Transportation Economics, 33*(1), 51–58.

Hayut, Y. (1981). Containerization and the load center concept. *Economic Geography, 57*(2), 160–176.

Heaver, T., Meersman, H., & Van De Voorde, E. (2001). Co-operation and competition in international container transport: Strategies for ports. *Maritime Policy & Management, 28*(3), 293–305.

Hoshino, H. (2010). Competition and collaboration among container ports. *The Asian Journal of Shipping and Logistics, 26*(1), 31–47.

Jans, T. (2016). *The impact of geographical clusters on environmental strategies* (Ph.D. thesis defended in February 2016, Vrije Universiteit Brussel, Brussels).

Lavie, D. (2006). The competitive advantage of interconnected firms: An extension of the resource-based view. *Academy of Management Review, 31*(3), 638–658.

Marlow, P. B., & Paixao, A. C. (2001). Agility, a key enabler in port competition. In International Association of Maritime Economists (Eds.), *Annual Conference Proceeding* (pp. 102–114). Hong Kong: Polytechnic University—Depterment of Shipping and Transport Logistics.

McEvily, B., & Zaheer, A. (1999). Bridging ties: A source of firm heterogeneity in competitive capabilities. *Strategic Management Journal, 20*(12), 133–1156.

Notteboom, T. E., & Rodrigue, J. P. (2005). Port regionalization: Towards a new phase in port development. *Maritime Policy & Management, 32*(3), 297–313.

Notteboom, T., & Winkelmans, W. (2001). Structural changes in logistics: How do port authorities face the challenge? *Maritime Policy & Management, 28*, 71–89.

Notteboom, T., & Winkelmans, W. (2004). Overall market dynamics and their influence on the port sector (Factual Report—Work Package 1 FR-WP1). Brussels: European Sea Ports Organisation the Notion of Dry Ports. *Maritime Economics & Logistics, 14*(1) (2012), 14–32.

Porter, M. E. (1990). *The competitive advantage of nations*. New York: Free Press.

Porter, M. E. (2000). Location, competition, and economic development: Local clusters in a global economy. *Economic Development Quarterly, 14*(1), 15–34.

Robinson, R. (2002). Ports as elements in value-driven chain systems: The new paradigm. *Maritime Policy & Management, 29*(3), 241–255.

Rodrigue, J.-P. (2010). Maritime transportation: Drivers for the shipping and port industries. In International Transport Forum: ITF (2010), *Highlights of the international transport forum 2010: Transport and innovation: Unleashing the potential.* Paris: OECD Publishing. http://dx.doi.org/10.1787/itf_highlights-2010-en.

Rodrigue, J.-P., & Notteboom, T. (2009). The terminalization of supply chains: Reassessing the role of terminals in port/hinterland logistical relationships. *Maritime Policy & Management, 36*(2), 165–183.

Rodrigue, J.-P., Comtois, C., & Slack, B. (2009). *The geography of transport systems*. Routledge: Hofstra University, Department of Global Studies & Geography.

Roso, V., Woxenius, J., & Lumsden, K. (2009). The dry port concept: Connecting container seaports with the hinterland. *Journal of Transport Geography, 17*(5), 338–345.

Slack, B. (1985). Containerization, inter port competition and port selection. *Maritime Policy & Management, 5*(12), 293–303.

Song, D.-W. (2003). Port co-opetition in concept and in practice. *Maritime Policy & Management, 30*(1), 29–44.

Song, D.-W., & Panayides, P. M. (2008). Global supply chain and port/terminal: Integration and competitiveness. *Maritime Policy & Management, 35*(1), 73–87.

Suárez-Alemán, A., Serebrisky, T., & Ponce De León, O. (2017). Port competition in Latin America and the Caribbean: The role of concessions and competition policy. *Maritime Policy & Management, 45*(5), 1–19.

Teece, D. J., Pisano, G., & Shuen, A. (1997). Dynamic capabilities and strategic management. *Strategic Management Journal, 18*(7), 509–533.

Teng, J. Y., Huang, W. C., & Huang, M. J. (2004). Multicriteria evaluation for port competitiveness of eight East Asian container ports. *Journal of Marine Science and Technology, 12*(4), 256–264.

UNCTAD (United Nations Conference on Trade and Development). (1982). *Multimodal transport and trade facilitation*. Geneva: UNCTAD.

Van den Berg, R., & De Langen, P. W. (2011). Hinterland strategies of port authorities: A case study of the Port of Barcelona. *Research in Transportation Economics, 33*, 6–14.

Van Der Horst, M. R., & De Langen, P. W. (2008). Coordination in hinterland transport chains: A major challenge for the seaport community. *Maritime Economics & Logistics, 10*(1–2), 108–129.

van der Horst, M. R., & van der Lugt, L. M. (2011). Coordination mechanisms in improving hinterland accessibility: Empirical analysis in the port of Rotterdam. *Maritime Policy & Management, 38*(4), 415–435.

Veenstra, A., Zuidwijk, R., & van Asperen, E. (2012). The extended gate concept for container terminals: Expanding the notion of dry ports. *Maritime Economics & Logisticsn, 14*(1), 14–32.

Verhoeven, P. (2009). European ports policy: Meeting contemporary governance challenges. *Maritime Policy & Management, 36*(1), 79–101.

Wan, Y., Zhang, A., & Li, K. X. (2018). Port competition with accessibility and congestion: A theoretical framework and literature review on empirical studies. *Maritime Policy & Management, 45*(2), 239–259.

Wang, J. J., & Slack, B. (2004). Regional governance of port development in China: A case study of Shanghai International Shipping Center. *Maritime Policy & Management, 31*(4), 357–373.

Wassmer, U., & Dussauge, P. (2011). Value creation in alliance portfolios: The benefits and costs of network resource interdependencies. *European Management Review, 8*(1), 47–64.

Wernerfelt, B. (1984). A resource-based view of the firm. *Strategic Management Journal, 52*, 171–180.

Wilmsmeier, G., Monios, J., & Lambert, B. (2011). The directional development of intermodal freight corridors in relation to inland terminals. *Journal of Transport Geography, 19*, 1379–1386.

World Bank. (2007). *The evolution of ports in a competitive world in 2007*. Washington, DC: The World Bank.

Xing, W., Liu, Q., & Chen, G. (2018). Pricing strategies for port competition and cooperation. *Maritime Policy & Management, 45*(2), 260–277.

Yap, W. Y., & Lam, J. S. (2004). An interpretation of inter-container port relationships from the demand perspective. *Maritime Policy & Management, 31*(4), 337–355.

5

The Impact of Clusters on Firms' Environmental Strategies: Case Study of Antwerp's Chemical Cluster

Tim Jans and Elvira Haezendonck

Corporate social responsibility (CSR) has gone through incremental changes during the last decades (Carroll 1999). The importance of the environmental component of CSR increased during this evolution. Initially, firms limited their actions to product innovations that reduce the final product's environmental impact. This gradually evolved to process innovations, improving production processes and logistical systems. A new phase commenced when firms sought improvements beyond their own firm boundaries and collaborated vertically with their partners in the supply chain. The firms evaluated the environmental impact of their products during their whole life cycle to reduce these products' environmental damage. A more recent and less discussed phenomenon is horizontal collaboration between firms. Firms seek environmental

---

T. Jans
Vrije Universiteit Brussel (VUB), Brussels, Belgium

E. Haezendonck (✉)
Department of Business, Vrije Universiteit Brussel (VUB), Brussels, Belgium
e-mail: elvira.haezendonck@vub.be

E. Haezendonck and A. Verbeke (eds.), *Sustainable Port Clusters and Economic Development*, Palgrave Studies in Maritime Economics,
https://doi.org/10.1007/978-3-319-96658-8_5

improvements in collaborative initiatives with competitors. Sharing resources, capabilities, and competencies are ways of building jointly on new competitive advantages.

A geographical cluster is an excellent instrument for this type of collaboration. Cluster collaboration is often coordinated and/or facilitated by cluster organizations, and can induce firm-specific advantages, in this case termed cluster-specific advantages. This paper focuses on the impact of clusters on the development of green cluster-specific advantages. Research into the level of collaboration in a cluster and the development process of green cluster-specific advantages is valuable information for policymakers, because these advantages improve firms' environmental strategies. Furthermore this information is beneficial for the cluster firms, because green cluster-specific advantages can generate a competitive advantage relative to firms outside the cluster.

Hart (1995) described the development process of green capabilities, taking a resource-based perspective. His natural resource-based view states that investments in five resource domains (Verbeke et al. 2006) will foster the growth of green capabilities, which can generate a competitive advantage for the firm (Hart 1995). Verbeke et al. (2006) build on Hart's (1995) work by constructing an integrated framework, adding the organizational context to Hart's (1995) conceptual model. This organizational context consists of the influencing factors of the proactivity of environmental strategies on the micro-level. Next to these factors, some papers discuss macro-level factors (e.g., Porter and Van der Linde 1995). Jans et al. (2015) pointed at the need to include the meso-level in this context, too. The meso-level is a level in-between, focusing on collaborative relationships and collaboration entities. It studies how a group of firms as a higher order entity, as one "system," improve their joint and individual strategic positions. Investments in more proactive environmental strategies may, for example, be influenced by the industry or sector of the firm or by their networks. The firm can develop such a network in a geographical cluster, if it is located in one. Dyer and Sing (1998) described how shared resources can generate a competitive advantage. The natural resource-based view of Hart (1995) can be extended by incorporating inter-firm resources, as described by Dyer and Sing (1998) and suggested by Lavie (2006). These inter-firm resources, whether or not in combination with firm-specific resources, may generate green capabilities. If these are valuable, rare, non-imitable, and non-substitutable (Barney 1991), they can result in a competitive advantage for the firm.

This paper focuses on clusters and cluster organizations. We elaborate a case study about the petrochemical and chemical cluster in the Antwerp port. The aim of this study is to determine whether the cluster contributes to the proactivity of the cluster firms' environmental strategies, and if so, how this happens. We study the facilitating role of the cluster for its firms and explore the extent to which the cluster contributes to a more proactive environmental strategy.

The next section explains the methodology of this study. We peruse the literature about clusters and cluster life cycles in Sect. 3. In Sect. 4, the case study of the Antwerp petrochemical and chemical cluster is elaborated. The cluster is defined, and the cluster organizations and their roles are described. Some cluster organizations are discussed more extensively, because they are more than others involved in dealing with environmental issues. Furthermore, we identify and discuss a number of specific environmental accomplishments. Finally, we perform an analysis of the cluster life cycle to identify a number of complexities that point at some gaps in the literature up to now. The last section contains the conclusions of this study.

1 Methodology

The aim of this study is to determine whether the cluster contributes to the proactivity of the cluster firms' environmental strategies, and if so, how this happens. Therefore, we do a case study of the petrochemical and chemical cluster in the Antwerp port. First, we study the literature about clusters and environmental strategies and how they can be integrated into the natural resource-based view (Hart 1995). Furthermore, we also study relevant literature about networks and inter-firm collaboration, and its integration into the extended natural resource-based view (Lavie 2006). In addition, we peruse literature about cluster life cycles. In a second step, we study the Antwerp petrochemical and chemical cluster by performing six in-depth interviews with managers and/or presidents from local cluster organizations that coordinate and/or facilitate collaboration between cluster firms. We also studied a large number of documents, such as annual reports from cluster organizations and reports and information brochures from Essenscia, the industry association.

Based on all this information, we first describe the most important cluster organizations and their role for the cluster. Next, we show a number of cluster projects that show the cluster's environmental contribution. In a following step, we create a timeline with important events and decisions that had a significant impact on the cluster, and we describe the cluster's life cycle. With this step, we intend to clarify how the cluster has arrived at its current point in which it functions as a good platform for environmental inter-firm collaboration.

2 Clusters and the Natural Resource-Based View

2.1 Cluster Theories

We identified several cluster theories in the existing cluster literature. Clusters can be studied from the perspective of location theory (classical,[1] neo-classical,[2] and modern[3]) industrial organization theory,[4] transaction cost theory,[5] industrial districts theory,[6] and the systems of innovation approach[7] (Muizer and Hospers 2000). The two most cited

[1]Location decisions are taken based on transport costs.

[2]In addition to transport costs, also location interdependence and the market is taken into account.

[3]The modern location theory assumes that managers are satisfied with sub-optimal decisions. The theory of Krugman (1991) takes this perspective.

[4]The industrial organization theory assumes an imperfect market and uses collaboration against market failures.

[5]Each transaction causes transaction costs, which should be taken into account when making decisions.

[6]See Porter's (2000) definition.

[7]Innovation is a learning process requiring interaction and collaboration with other organizations.

theories are from Porter (1998, 2000) and Krugman (1991) (Hoen 2001; Roh 2007). Porter (1998, 2000) regards clusters as physically proximate organizations in the same or related sectors, linked by vertical or horizontal relations. On the other hand, Krugman (1991) takes a more macroeconomic perspective and describes how self-reinforcing economic activities increase the welfare and growth of regions.

Because Porter's (2000) definition takes a more micro- and meso-focused perspective, it is more suited for this paper. "Clusters are geographic concentrations of interconnected companies, specialized suppliers, service providers, firms in related industries, and associated institutions (e.g., universities, standards agencies, trade associations) in a particular field that compete but also cooperate" (Porter 2000: 15). A definition taking a resource-based perspective states that "[c]lusters are non-random geographical agglomerations of firms with similar or highly complementary capabilities" (Maskell and Lorenzen 2004: 1002). In other words, firms with similar capabilities, in most cases competitors, or firms with highly complementary capabilities, i.e., suppliers, clients, or competitors, are often attracted to the same geographical area for several reasons discussed in the next paragraph. On the other hand, firms in the same geographical area tend to develop similar or highly complementary capabilities. As explained by Hart's (1995) resource-based view, capabilities are developed based on resources. The extended resource-based view explains that part of a firm's resources can be shared resources. For example, a geographical cluster develops a joint resource base over time, out of which cluster firms can tap resources, depending on their activeness in local cluster organizations or in other platforms in which local inter-firm contacts are supported. Because the shared resources are more or less the same for the cluster firms, they tend to develop similar or highly complementary capabilities.

3 Cluster Advantages

Fierce competition in a cluster improves cluster firms' performances (Porter 1998). Folta et al. (2006) looked at the impact of cluster size on cluster firms' innovation rate, alliance partners, and private investors.

They found increasing individual performances until the cluster consisted of about 65 firms, after which the effect reversed. Decarolis and Deeds (1999) observed a positive link between cluster membership and the firm's financial performance. According to Porter (1998), competition and collaboration arise simultaneously in a cluster, but between different firms. However, in our case study, we did observe firms that compete and collaborate at the same time with the same partners.

Clusters generate a competitive advantage because they increase productivity, stimulate innovation, and attract new firms (Porter 1998, 2000; Marshall 1920). Other advantages of cluster membership are an increased likelihood that the firm internationalizes and, hence, higher international sales (Fernhaber et al. 2003). However, Porter (1998) indicated that a cluster needs at least ten years to establish a certain depth and create a competitive advantage.

3.1 Cluster-Specific Advantages

Verbeke et al.'s (2006) conceptual framework, which is based on Hart's (1995) work, explains that specific internal organization parameters (on the micro-level) have an impact on the environmental investments in five resource domains: (1) conventional green competences, (2) green employee skills, (3) green organizational competences, (4) formal environmental management systems and procedures, and (5) the reconfiguration of the strategic planning process. Investments in proactive environmental strategies enhance the development of firm-specific capabilities, i.e., higher order learning, stakeholder integration, and continuous innovation. These capabilities may generate a competitive advantage (Hart 1995; Sharma and Vredenburg 1998; Verbeke et al. 2006). In addition to these studies, research has been done to macro-level factors influencing environmental strategies, i.e., country-specific advantages (inter alia Porter and Van der Linde 1995; Esty and Porter 2002). Esty and Porter (2002) find a significant positive relation between a country's environmental performance and environmental regulation. An extensive literature review of all micro-level and macro-level influencing factors can be found in Jans et al. (2015). They argue that these influencing factors can also stem from the meso-level. Advantages stemming from clusters can be called cluster-specific advantages. Verbeke and Vanden Bussche (2005) discuss alliance-specific advantages and compare these with subsidiary-specific advantages (Rugman and Verbeke 2001). According to the authors, the difference is "that the relevant knowledge base is not embedded within the subsidiary but within the alliance" (Verbeke and Vanden Bussche 2005: 127). For cluster-specific advantages, the knowledge base is embedded in the cluster, i.e., in the local cluster organizations. This embeddedness refers to the idea that firms' economic actions are shaped by the structure and quality of social ties in an inter-firm network, because these ties create unique opportunities and access to these opportunities (Uzzi 1996). In other words, local cluster organizations are actors supporting cluster development because they are an excellent vehicle to enhance inter-firm ties in a geographical cluster, which leads to business opportunities for the firms involved in the cluster organizations. Cluster organizations can be created for a specific task, or they can be existing organizations used for cluster development, such as a Chamber of Commerce.

3.2 A Resource-Based Perspective of Cluster-Specific Advantages

When collaborating via a cluster organization, firms share resources. This way they create a knowledge base in the cluster organization. Bleischwitz and Thomas (2007) speak of "resource-dependent relations". They notice that it is important that each firm should have an interest in the access to the other firms' resources. If firms collaborate to create superior value by combining their resources (cf. Dyer and Singh's [1998] relational view), they will develop capabilities that may generate firm-specific advantages (Verbeke and Vanden Bussche 2005), termed cluster-specific advantages if obtained via cluster collaboration. McEviley and Zaheer (1999: 1152) stated that "a firm's configuration of linkages with other actors in the cluster is an important vehicle through which the firm's skills, competencies, and routines are continually upgraded, refreshed, and renewed." Prahalad and Hamel (1990: 82) stated that "[un]like physical assets, which do deteriorate over time, competencies are enhanced as they are applied and shared". This also points to the existence of collaborative advantages. Hart's (1995) natural resource-based view applies this reasoning to the development of green firm-specific advantages; resources (in this case shared resources) lead to investments in several resource domains, which, on their turn, generate the development of eco-friendly capabilities. If a capability is valuable, rare, non-imitable, and non-substitutable (Barney 1991), it becomes a firm-specific competency that produces a sustainable firm-specific advantage. In this case, such an advantage may be called a cluster-specific advantage, as it is built on shared resources from the cluster's knowledge base. A sustainable advantage may consist of a cost advantage or a product differentiation advantage, or it can be a reinforcement of a firm's future market position (Sharma and Vredenburg 1998; Verbeke et al. 2006).

3.3 Cluster Life Cycle

A cluster passes through several stages during its existence. The cluster life cycle was discussed by Porter (1998), Van Klink and De Langen (2001), Swann (2002), Wolter (2003), Maggioni (2004), Maskell and Kebir (2005), Bergman (2006, 2008), and Menzel and Fornahl (2010). Most authors identified four stages in the cluster life cycle. This paper uses Van Klink and De Langen's (2001) terminology for the cluster life stages: development, expansion, maturation, and transition or decline. Maskell and Kebir (2005) use three stages and leave out the maturation stage. They tend to believe that the maturation stage is not really a stage, but a moment in time, during which the balance shifts from growth (expansion) to decline. However, we believe that the maturation phase can be a stable and long enduring stage, and our case study further in this paper confirms this point of view.

A cluster will emerge in a location where several firms develop superior routines (Menzel and Fornahl 2010). In this stage the firms' market relations develop, creating a value chain. The first signs of collaboration are observed. Success factors are a strong local demand and a large local resource and knowledge base, drawing more firms to the cluster (Van Klink & De Langen 2001). The geographical proximity of other firms is of high importance for the transfer of tacit technology. In this phase, the cluster grows slowly until it reaches a critical mass. Once reached, growth soars (Swann 2002), and the cluster reaches the expansion stage.

In the expansion stage, further growth occurs in this stage because the cluster firms start to explore new markets. Therefore, risk capital is of high importance (Van Klink and De Langen 2001). Geographic proximity remains important for tacit knowledge transfers (Swann 2002). Maggioni (2004) identifies eight growth stimulators of a cluster: (1) spin-offs of existing firms and imitation by new firms, (2) the profit potential demonstrated by the present firms, (3) the positive impact on a firm's quality reputation when locating in an area with increased competition, (4) the diffusion of information along potential entrants about the profit potential of a specific location, (5) the contribution to cluster development of a large established firm, (6) the growth of the number of small subcontractors providing services or products to the large and/or leading firms in the cluster, (7) a decreasing rejection of new firms, thus the disappearance of the "fight for legitimacy," once a critical mass is obtained, and (8) cluster economies, such as a labor market pool. We notice that not all potential clusters reach the expansion stage. To reach this phase, the heterogeneity between the firms should not be too large, because the cluster needs a focal point. On the other hand, a minimum of diversity is required to generate new ideas in the cluster and induce further growth (Menzel and Fornahl 2010). As an example, we refer to Orsenigo (2001), who studied a potential biotechnology cluster in Italy and concluded that it did not reach the expansion stage because, among other reasons, the heterogeneity of the firms was too large.

During the maturation stage, the importance of geographical proximity diminishes because knowledge becomes more codified. This means that tacit knowledge becomes more scarce because it is increasingly replaced by explicit knowledge. "*Tacit knowledge is subconsciously understood and applied, difficult to articulate, developed from direct experience and action, and usually shared through highly interactive conversation, story-telling and shared experience. Explicit knowledge, in contrast, can be more precisely and formally articulated*" (Zack 1999: 46). Tacit knowledge is replaced by explicit knowledge by codifying the knowledge, i.e., by organizing, categorizing or documenting it, making it easier to transfer or share it. As a consequence, physical proximity to related firms becomes less important, and the cluster's attractiveness for new firms reduces or disappears (Swann 2002). In addition, because knowledge becomes easier accessible outside the cluster, competition intensifies during this stage. A number of firms attain a dominant position in the cluster. Furthermore, the cluster develops a global dimension, i.e., firms lose their focus on the local market, internationalize and possibly create subsidiaries in other countries (Van Klink and De Langen 2001). Bergman (2006) states that the cluster enters the maturation stage when it loses the capability of adapting to the changing market.

The final stage is often called the declining stage. Van Klink and De Langen (2001) termed this stage the transition stage, because two possible scenarios can unfold. The cluster can fall into a downward spiral, causing the cluster to disappear. Another possibility is that the cluster will go through a transition; new collaborative initiatives are initiated with existing or new firms. This results in new competences averting the downward spiral. In addition, it rejuvenates the cluster by bringing it back to a previous stage. Tappi (2005) performed a case study of the accordion cluster in Marche (Italy), which used its existing capabilities and knowledge to successfully transfer into an electronics cluster. Swann (2002) describes two causes of a cluster's decline. Firms in the cluster's originating industries disappear because the industry life cycle reaches its end. At the same time, the cluster fails to attract a sufficient number of new entrants in new industries. Grabher (1993) and Hassink and Shin (2005) found three causes of a cluster's decline. The cluster can suffer from a functional lock-in, i.e., when the exchange relations are overly embedded, resulting in overspecialization and hence functional shortcomings. A cognitive lock-in implies that firms fail to recognize the cyclical downturn. Finally, a cluster may decline due to a political lock-in. This occurs when politicians concentrate too much on protecting the traditional industrial structures and hence curb the cluster's modernization.

The cluster's internal collaborative relations go through a number of changes during the cluster's life cycle. In the development stage, collaboration is limited to R&D and the development of joint routines and standardization procedures. During the expansion stage, also collaborative initiatives for employee training and marketing arise, as well as initiatives to exploit scale economies. During the maturation stage, the firms do not undertake any additional collaborative initiatives. Finally, in the transition stage, new collaborative initiatives are important to avert the downward spiral and obtain new competences (Van Klink and De Langen 2001).

We note that the changing cluster characteristics throughout their life cycle are based on qualitative studies. Audretsch (1987) did an empirical analysis of firm properties throughout the industry life cycle, and concluded that the level of R&D, the employees' skills and a firm's capital intensity are a good proxy for determining the stage in which the firm is situated. Unfortunately, such an analysis was not performed for the cluster life cycle.

4 The Petrochemical and Chemical Cluster in the Antwerp Port

4.1 Origin and Importance of the Cluster

After World War Two, the Antwerp port profited by the Marshall plan. Especially since 1960, growth soared. During the early 60s, the Antwerp city developed a large area north of the city for petrochemical and chemical activities. This successfully attracted a large number of firms. Nowadays, a third of the Belgian chemical industry is located in the Antwerp port. It is the second largest petrochemical cluster in the world considering its production volume, only surpassed by the cluster in Houston, Texas (Kamer van Koophandel Antwerpen-Waasland 2003). The Antwerp petrochemical sector generates 24.000 full-time jobs and is indirectly responsible for another 20.000–40.000 full-time equivalents (Kamer van Koophandel Antwerpen-Waasland 2003) in supplier firms (transport, storage, construction, maintenance, etc.) and service firms (insurances, legal assistance, catering, security firms, etc.).

4.2 Cluster Boundaries

As discussed before, the cluster definition is not unequivocal. Geographical proximity is a relative concept. In the USA, cluster firms can be separated by a one-day travel time. In Europe, this is more or less limited to an hour (Sainsbury 1999). Furthermore, Porter (2000) points at the importance of identifying the internal links and complementarities to determine the cluster boundaries. The petrochemical and chemical firms in Antwerp, Terneuzen (Dow Chemical) and Geel (i.e., BP and Ineos) can be regarded as one cluster. BASF in Antwerp and Dow Chemical in Terneuzen are competitors, as well as collaborators. When one of these firms loses production capacity due to a problem or maintenance, the competitor's capacity loss is taken care of by increasing one's own production. In addition, the number of joint investment projects is growing. The Antwerp cluster is also connected with the clusters in Rotterdam and Moerdijk via the RAPL (Rotterdam-Antwerp Pipeline). Hence, it is possible to consider Rotterdam's chemical firms as part of the cluster. The central position of Antwerp in the extensive European petrochemical pipeline network is shown in Fig. 1. This network will be further extended throughout the whole of Europe in the near future. Hence, we can state that all firms connected to the pipeline network form one cluster. In addition to this, Porter (2000) also includes supporting institutions in the cluster, such as universities, standard agencies, and trade associations. The University of Antwerp has indeed been involved in "Routeplan 2012," a project to develop the cluster further.

Based on the perceived mutual links between firms, we can identify a large and a small petrochemical and chemical cluster, as shown in Fig. 1. The large cluster (dotted line) includes the firms in the Antwerp port, the Geel-Tessenderlo area, the area Ghent-Terneuzen and the firms in Rotterdam. In this cluster, only operational collaboration is observed. For example, we can observe long pipelines for a number of main chemical products between these locations. However, contacts and discussions between and joint decision making of firms in

Fig. 1 The European pipeline network and the small and large clusters (*Source* Port of Antwerp, 2005)

different countries or regions are limited to nonexistent. The small cluster (solid line) only includes the firms in the Antwerp port. Especially in the last years, more strategic collaborative initiatives take place, e.g., via the Routeplan 2012 project. A number of collaboration coordinating organizations is exclusively or almost exclusively active in collaborative projects with firms in the Antwerp port. An example is the organization VIBNA, an organization allowing regular informal contacts between the chemical firms located in the Antwerp port area. Because strategic collaboration can only be found in the small cluster, it is chosen as the object of this case study.

4.3 The Small Cluster

The Antwerp petrochemical and chemical cluster includes the chemical sector, the petrochemical sector, the petroleum sector and service firms such as maintenance and logistic firms. These cluster firms have equal or complementary capabilities, in line with Maskell and Lorenzen's (2004) cluster definition. Most customer-supplier relationships are very intense and hence of strategic importance. Furthermore the cluster firms are connected by more than 100 pipelines, taking care of 52% of the internal transport.

The Antwerp cluster includes five refineries. They produce petroleum products out of crude oil. Two large refineries, one of Total and one of ExxonMobil, are connected to the RAPL. The three smaller ones are operated by Petroplus. Furthermore, the cluster includes four oil crackers, producing ethylene and propylene, vital for the petrochemical sector. One is operated by BASF, and the other three belong to Fina Antwerp Olefins, a joint venture of Total and ExxonMobil. These basic products are further processed by the firms into a huge number of different chemical products. Finally, the cluster includes the aforementioned service firms.

As argued before, attracting new firms is a valuable asset of clusters (Porter 1998). Hinterland access in one of the important factors impacting firms' location decisions (Kreukels and Wever 1998). The Antwerp port and the local infrastructure have indeed fostered the Antwerp cluster's growth. The cluster has an extensive internal pipeline network and is connected to the European network as well (Fig. 1). In addition, a large number of suppliers and service providers are located in the area. Furthermore, the cluster is connected to the European railway and canal network, allowing quick access to important industrial areas in Germany, the Netherlands, France, and Switzerland (Port of Antwerp, 2005). Improvements to the local road system are in preparation. In addition to this infrastructure and multimodal accessibility, the Antwerp port also offers cost reductions, easier risk management and a higher innovation potential.

4.4 A Life Cycle Analysis of the Antwerp Cluster

Figure 2 shows a timeline depicting local events and decisions with a substantial impact on the petrochemical and chemical cluster in the Antwerp port. The cluster originated in the early 60s. At the end of the same decade, the first collaborative initiative could be observed. This collaboration resulted in the founding of VIBNA in 1973, establishing a permanent collaborative structure. During the next decades, coordination of collaborative initiatives shifted now and then to other cluster organizations, depending on the needs of the firms and the specific collaboration topics. Local themes, such as air or water quality, were dealt with by the local cluster organization VIBNA until 2002. However, this organization refocused, and these issues are now coordinated by VOKA Grootindustrie, a subdivision of the local Chamber of Commerce. Environmental issues surpassing the local level, such as legislative issues, are discussed on the regional level, as Flanders is responsible

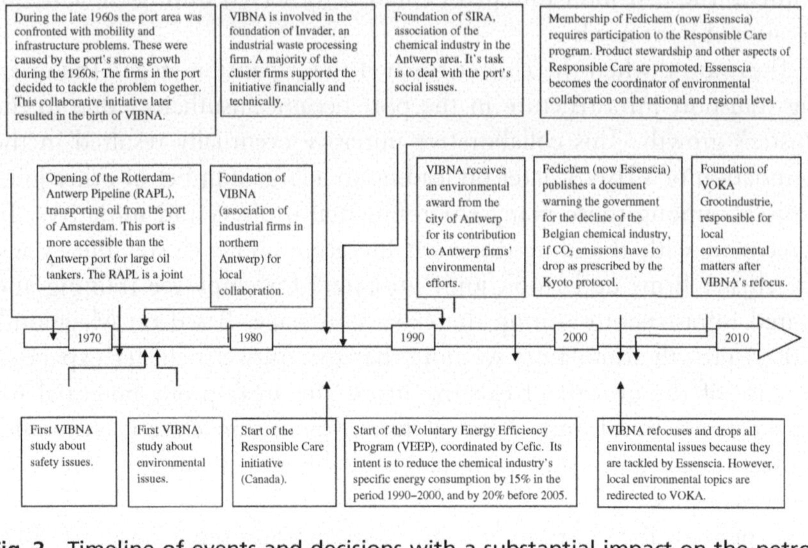

Fig. 2 Timeline of events and decisions with a substantial impact on the petrochemical and chemical cluster in Antwerp

for environmental legislation. These issues are coordinated by Essencia Flanders, before 2007 called Fedichem.

Clusters can emerge in two ways: policy-driven or spontaneous (Su and Hung 2009). As mentioned before, the Antwerp cluster originated during the early 60s. The local government reserved a large area north of the city for petrochemical and chemical firms. The cluster developed in a way up to now neglected in the literature; it was almost exclusively based on alluring existing petrochemical and chemical firms to the area. These large firms situated a new production plant in the Antwerp port because of the local authorities' initiative. Therefore, the development stage of this cluster has other characteristics than described in the literature (see Sect. 2 of this paper). The cluster firms did not build exclusively on local resources such as cheap land. On the contrary, they used resources and know-how of the multinational's parent firm. They also obtained environmental knowledge and skills via this parent firm. Although the firms developed market relationships, a substantive part of the value chain was still situated outside the cluster. Collaboration was limited. The first joint initiatives could be observed during the late 60s because of joint needs.

These arose when the cluster reached the expansion stage. The existing transport infrastructure in the port became insufficient due to the cluster's growth. This collaborative initiative eventually resulted in the foundation of VIBNA, later on leading to a large number of other joint projects, among those many environmental projects and initiatives. In agreement with the afore-discussed literature about cluster life cycles, the cluster firms undertook joint initiatives for employee training and shared infrastructure during the expansion stage. Based on Maggioni's (2004) growth stimulators we note that the Antwerp cluster expanded because of the growth of existing firms, the area's profit potential for new petrochemical and chemical firms, increasing cluster economies (infrastructure and other resources) and the growth of the number of subcontractors.

At present, the cluster is still in the maturation stage. Swann (2002) stated that a cluster reaches this stage when the cluster's shared knowledge becomes more codified, losing attractiveness for new firms. For the Antwerp cluster the reduced attractiveness is mainly due to changes in the cluster's environment. This is discussed in a document of the local Chamber of Commerce of 2006. Some examples are the situation of the local road infrastructure, the evolution of labor costs, continually stricter environmental regulations, etc. We note that even during the maturation phase, the firms still do not engage in joint R&D projects. According to the cluster life cycle literature (see Sect. 2), joint R&D projects usually arise during the cluster's early stages. In petrochemical and chemical firms, a majority of R&D projects are carried out by the parent firms. The resulting knowledge is of strategic importance and, hence, not shared with other firms. Furthermore, the cluster life cycle literature describes a cluster's development process from a local orientation in the development stage to a shared local and global orientation in the maturation stage. Contrary to this literature, we observe a global orientation in the development stage, i.e., the cluster firms made use of their parent firms' knowledge and skills and market relations were limited. This evolved into a shared local and global orientation in the maturation stage, partially as a result of the large number of collaborative cluster projects. Another observation is that there is no increased pressure on the strategic relations during the maturation stage, though this is mentioned in the afore-described literature. However, this literature is mainly based on clusters originating out of new firms, and does not take into account clusters based on multinationals. Although competition does exist between the subsidiaries in the cluster, its direct impact is limited. As a consequence, pressure on the firms' strategic relations during the maturation stage is limited, too. Furthermore, collaboration becomes more easy.

The Antwerp cluster has not (yet) reached the declining stage. Swann (2002) states that a chemical cluster is not likely to disappear. It is an industry generating a large number of spillovers for many other industries. In case the cluster should reach the declining stage, related industries would ensure its continuation.

The above description of the cluster's life cycle shows that reality is more complex than described in cluster literature up to now. The first complexity is that existing literature described in this paper's second section mainly focuses on clusters that developed spontaneously. This was also argued by Su and Hung (2009). These authors did a case study of a spontaneous biotechnology cluster and compared it with a policy-driven one. They described the huge difference throughout these clusters' life cycles. Martin and Sunley (2006) and Menzel and Fornahl (2010) indicate that a lot of authors discuss "coincidences" leading to a cluster's birth. However, in many of these cases, the cluster is the result of a strategic intent.

The fact that the cluster developed out of multinationals' subsidiaries, not out of new firms, strengthens the cluster's deviation of the standard life cycle. We could not find a study that describes this category of clusters. These clusters deserve more attention in future studies, as this complexity is the basis for the three following complexities.

A third complexity is that the firms did not rely exclusively on local resources during the cluster's early stages. On the contrary, they used their parent firms' resources and know-how and, hence, did not have to build up a completely new firm. However, we notice that the firms did evolve toward an orientation comparable to firms in the more traditionally described clusters. The latter progress from a local orientation toward a combined local and global orientation. The Antwerp cluster firms advanced from a global orientation toward a combined one; they still rely on their parent firms' resources, but make use of the local resource base, too.

Another complexity implies that the firms collaborate on other areas than traditionally described clusters. In the Antwerp cluster, we could not observe joint R&D projects. Marketing is another activity that is not tackled collectively. However, the firms do exchange a lot of knowledge and skills, mainly via informal contacts. They developed a number of shared routines and have joint employee training programs, especially concerning safety issues.

In a cluster the pressure on the firms' strategic relations increases during the maturation stage, because of the increased competitive forces. The fifth and last complexity is that we could not observe this phenomenon in the Antwerp cluster. Because the majority of cluster firms are production plants of multinationals, the direct impact of increased competitive forces is less noticeable for these firms; direct competition takes place between the firms' parent firms, while subsidiaries are more in competition with other subsidiaries of their own parent firm.

Therefore, no change in the strategic relations could be observed. On the contrary, collaborative initiatives are still thriving. This complexity results in more and better inter-firm collaboration in the cluster during the maturation stage.

The above complexities have an impact on the role of individual cluster actors on the one hand and on governments' role for the stimulation and facilitation of more proactive environmental strategies in specific on the other hand. Governments' role during a cluster's development stage has a huge impact on the cluster's characteristics. These characteristics influence the cluster's future development and the actors' possibilities to collaborate in the long term. More research into the diverse cluster categories, their specific characteristics and the required role of all actors involved is needed. However, we did already observe that this kind of cluster seems to be more suited for long-term collaboration, also throughout the later stages of the life cycle. It was shown that the cluster's collaboration differed from collaboration in more traditional clusters. It started later, but expanded quickly during the expansion stage. It is still ubiquitous in the maturation stage, as strategic relations suffered less from increased competition. The described collaborative projects in the cluster can be considered as illustrations of the intensity and effectiveness of the cluster's joint efforts.

5 Meso-Organisations Impacting the Antwerp Petrochemical and Chemical Cluster

Figure 3 provides an overview of meso-organisations exerting a direct or indirect influence on the petrochemical and chemical cluster in the Antwerp port. The depicted relations do not constitute an exhaustive list; they are merely an overview of the most important links. The organizations operate on a range of different geographical levels: international, European, national, regional, or local. We can state in general that meso-organisations with a narrower geographic scope exert the most direct influence. Therefore, we call these cluster organizations.

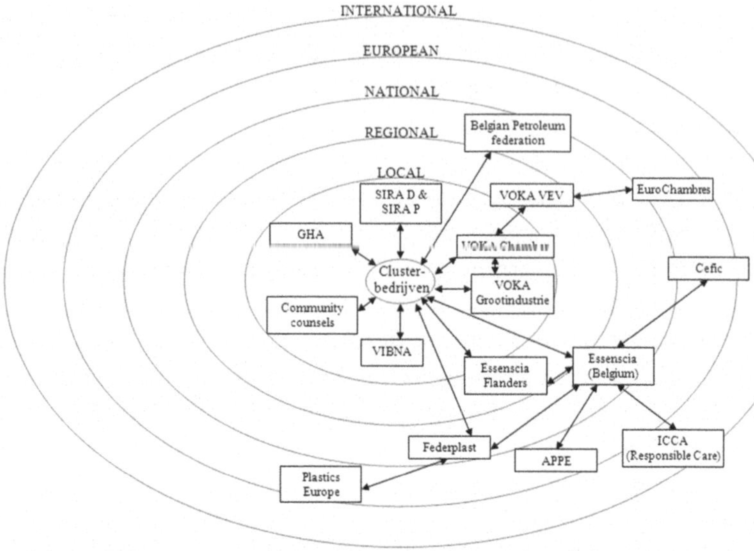

Fig. 3 Meso-organisations with an impact on the petrochemical and chemical cluster in Antwerp

Organizations with broader scopes mainly influence the cluster firms indirectly, often via the cluster organizations with a narrower scope. In this paragraph, we discuss all meso-organisations depicted in Fig. 3 that have a substantial impact on the cluster's collaborative environmental activities, i.e., Essenscia, VOKA, and VIBNA. The analyses of these cluster organizations and their mutual relation is based on relevant documents, such as annual reports and publications. In addition, we interviewed six important cluster actors. These highlighted the high degree of the cluster organizations' interwovenness. After all, all these organizations rely on more or less the same group of experts. This group, of about 15–20 people for the Antwerp cluster, consists of representatives of the largest cluster firms, in most cases the plant managers, and of representatives of some of the cluster organizations such as Essenscia and VOKA.

Essenscia: Essenscia is the Belgian sector association of the chemical and life sciences sector. Until May 2007, it was called Fedichem. It has three regional divisions: for Flanders, Wallonia, and Brussels.

These divisions deal with environmental issues because in Belgium regional governments are responsible for environmental legislation. Furthermore, Essenscia is involved in the implementation process of ICCA's Responsible Care project, a voluntary initiative of the chemical industry to improve its environmental performance. The organization compels participation to Responsible Care since 1991. It rewards original Responsible Care innovations, issues publications to facilitate Responsible Care implementation and organizes projects to improve smaller firms' performances by using larger firms' expertise. Furthermore, they assemble and analyze Responsible Care related data to show the industry's efforts during the past decades. This data shows great emission reductions between 1987 and 1993. However, since 1993, further reductions are more difficult. The firms have been successful in drastically reducing all waste products and emissions, except for CO_2. This is explained by huge investments during the 90s, in energy-intensive installations. In addition, this was accompanied by a significant increase of CO_2 as process emissions. Besides publications to encourage and support environmental initiatives, Essenscia (Fedichem) issued a document in 2002 warning the government for the closure of several chemical plants if it had to stick to the planned CO_2 reductions as prescribed by the Kyoto protocol. In the end, this has not been the result. The Kyoto targets for 2012 have not been met by reductions in Belgium. Instead, a large part of the reductions have been bought by carbon emission trading. This is because investments in other countries can result in stronger pollution reductions than the same investments in Belgium, as additional reductions become more and more expensive. According to a report of a Belgian NGO, 52% of the Belgian Kyoto emission reductions have been bought elsewhere, especially in India and China, for almost 200 million euro (Lamote 2013). Therefore, we cannot say whether Essenscia's claim was valid back in 2002, but if it was, they have found a way around it by means carbon emissions trading.

VOKA: VOKA is the association of Flemish Chambers of Commerce and the Flemish Economic Association (VEV). The Chambers operate independently, each responsible for local affairs in their area. The VEV deals with topics of regional or national importance, such as environmental legislation. VOKA has members across 24 sectors, providing 60% of Flemish private employment. The Chamber VOKA Antwerp-Waasland has about 3000 members. Their task is to look after the firms' affairs and to network for their members. In addition, they also provide some services for their members. VOKA Grootindustrie (Large industry) is a subdivision of the VOKA Antwerp-Waasland Chamber since 2003. It was founded to implement part of the Routeplan 2012 project to further develop the port area. Cluster collaborative initiatives involving VOKA are discussed within this subdivision's regular meetings.

In the past, VOKA was not involved in the discussions about environmental topics. In 2006 and 2007, they set up some initiatives with ENGOs (environmental NGOs). In addition, they were involved in the environmental policy formation process of GHA (the Antwerp municipal port enterprise). They try to avoid interference of GHA as an additional authority, because they fear that it will create local norms surpassing other ports' norms and, hence, undermine the Antwerp port's competitive position. Therefore, VOKA's definition of proactive environmental strategies is not to surpass the legislators' minimum demands. They only expect firms to look beyond current regulations, and to prepare for possible future stricter regulations. The port, hence GHA, should, according to VOKA, only play a facilitating role, not create additional rules. Furthermore the Chamber agrees that Kyoto can harm the Belgian chemical industry and the Belgian competitive position in Europe, because it argues that its impact on small countries is much larger than on large countries.

VIBNA: VIBNA is the association of industrial firms in northern Antwerp. It was founded in 1973 to formalize and embed the cluster firms' collaboration. This collaboration started when the Antwerp port suffered from severe accessibility problems, originated during the port's growth of the late 60s. At its foundation, VIBNA united 32 members from six sectors: automobile construction, electricity production, storage and transshipment, the metallurgical and ship repairing sector and finally two sectors of the cluster: the petroleum and chemical sectors. The exact number of members varied during the next decades. On average, 45% were chemical or petrochemical firms and 11% petroleum firms (VIBNA, annual reports 1987–2008). Hence, more than half of VIBNA members belong to Antwerp's petrochemical and chemical cluster.

VIBNA's goal is to bundle the firms' activities and efforts in dealing with local problems. The two most important subjects have long been safety and environment (VIBNA, annual report 1988). Their first safety initiative started in 1973. They created product and firm files with practical information for intervention teams and for the local community (VIBNA, annual report 1998). This initiative stemmed from the idea that a safety problem in one firm can also impact or damage the surrounding firms and population. Safety managers of collaborating firms met and still meet each other during regular gatherings to exchange best practices and knowledge. This collaboration generated improvements in all collaborating firms' safety performances. Figure 4 shows that the cluster's chemical firms and their subcontractors obtained a more significant drop in industrial accidents than other Belgian chemical firms outside the cluster.

Environmental collaborative initiatives were initially coordinated by VIBNA. This proved to be the most efficient solution in the former constellation of cluster organizations. According to a former president of VIBNA, the environmental topic arose when some Dutch organizations made accusations toward the cluster firms about water and

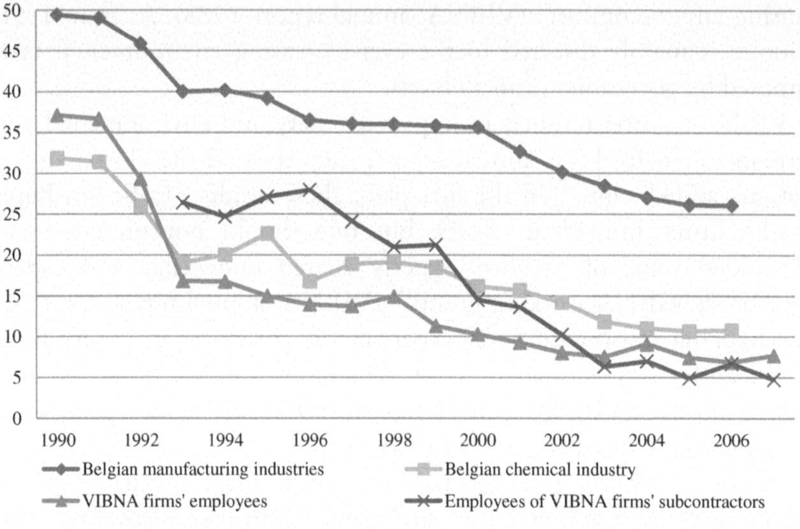

Fig. 4 Incidence rate of industrial accidents per million working hours

air pollution. A study, ordered by VIBNA, disproved the accusations, even stating that downstream water quality was better than up stream's. VIBNA also spurred the waste processing firm Indaver. Because safety (respect for human beings) and environmental responsibility (respect for the environment) are closely connected, local environmental topics continued to be VIBNA's responsibility for a long time. "One cannot obtain good results for the former, neglecting the latter" (VIBNA, annual report 1991: 4). Next to these topics, VIBNA also dealt with issues that were not managed by other cluster organizations, such as infrastructure, permits, industrial well-being, finances, and taxes (VIBNA, annual report 1993). However, safety and the environment remained VIBNA's main topics until 2002.

In VIBNA's annual reports up until 1996, they continually stressed the firms' efforts for environmental improvements. However, critique from governments and NGOs remained. They considered the government to be excessively repressive (VIBNA, annual report 1987); firms are too easily depicted as the main cause of environmental pollution (VIBNA, annual report 1987); and firms are excessively and inefficiently taxed (VIBNA, annual report 1990). Furthermore they state that "it is a utopia to think that industrial activities can expand without causing any discomfort" (VIBNA, annual report 1988). As from 1998, critique is mainly directed to the ever-increasing environmental taxes imposed by governments on all levels.

VIBNA's efforts resulted in improved safety and environmental performances. In its 1998 annual report, they stressed the cluster organization's added value: "In the first place these results can be attributed to the firms' individual efforts, but one should not underestimate the added value of the firm experts' shared knowledge and experience in all VIBNA working groups" (VIBNA, annual report 1998: 2). "Exchanging information and experience is enriching and contributes significantly to a permanent improvement of VIBNA firms' environmental policy" (VIBNA, annual report 1999: 10). Some examples of joint efforts are discussed further in this paper.

In 2002 VIBNA's goals changed. Essenscia was continually extending its working group activities and, hence, continually covering more environmental issues. The overlap with VIBNA's activities was growing. Therefore, VIBNA decided to leave these topics to Essenscia. Local environmental matters were redirected to VOKA Grootindustrie. After its refocus, they concentrated on safety management, industrial medicine, and operational environmental issues (VIBNA, annual report 2002). However, in practice the latter topic was dropped as well. This caused the complete disappearance of environmental topics in VIBNA's activities.

According to a former president of VIBNA, VIBNA's strength was the informal gatherings, giving the firms' managers the opportunity to find support, exchange information, and jointly deal with problems. A more formal structure was avoided, because it could undermine the organization's informal way of working. VIBNA's only formal body was a part-time secretariat. Apart from this part-time job, no one was paid directly by VIBNA. Every organization member paid for its representatives in VIBNA. In addition, this lack of structure made sure that only topics in line with the firms' needs were taken care of, and it kept costs low (about €500 per firm per year during the 80s, at present about €1500 per firm per year). Besides this small financial contribution, firms invest huge amounts of managerial time into the organization. The meetings consist of representatives, in most cases the plant managers, of the organization members. A former president of VIBNA states that VIBNA's return, especially in non-financial terms, is immense, mainly because of the shared know-how.

The RoutePlan 2012 Project: Routeplan 2012 is a joint project of multiple organizations with the goal to advance the economic position of the Antwerp-Waasland region. It is a white book describing a long-term vision for the region. First, the project introduces a number of initiatives to enhance growth in Antwerp's traditionally important sectors, i.e., transport and logistics, petrochemical, and diamond (Kamer van Koophandel Antwerpen-Waasland 2003). Later, the petrochemical domain was called "Large industries," to include other high-tech firms active in the region. A manager was hired by VOKA to coordinate and realize all initiatives of Routeplan 2012 within the platform "Large industries". The platform comprises about twenty large industrial firms from the Antwerp-Waasland region. Secondly, a number of initiatives are proposed to advance potential new growth sectors, i.e., (main) offices, tourism, and culture. A third part is about initiatives concerning completely new domains: the development of services for baby boomers and initiatives about product development, process optimization, and ICT/broadband. The last part of Routeplan 2012 focuses its attention on important side conditions to be worked on to be able to realize the initiatives of the first three parts. Some propositions are a better mobility plan, a stimulating tax system, and an appropriate spatial planning policy (Kamer van Koophandel Antwerpen-Waasland 2003). To realize the initiatives of the Routeplan 2012 project, existing meso-organizations, such as the Diamond High Council, or new meso-organizations, such as the platform "Large industries," were given responsibility for the coordination of specific initiatives. An example is the initiative concerning the enhancement of the mobility infrastructure in the region. Although this is a very sensitive and difficult issue for the region because of many different opinions and wishes for different stakeholders, decisions have been made and the structural mobility problems will be tackled. The manager of the platform "Large industries" is convinced that Routeplan 2012 is the ultimate proof of the added value of proactive initiatives on the meso-level.

6 Some Other Collaborative Initiatives in the Cluster

This paragraph describes a number of examples of joint initiatives and projects in the cluster, coordinated by one of the cluster organizations. We focus on initiatives with an environmental impact. Because of VIBNA's local importance for environmental initiatives until 2002, the majority of the projects were coordinated by VIBNA. The initiatives are shown in Table 1. The rows show which value chain activities (Porter 1998) profited from the initiative. The columns reveal whether the collaboration contributed to an improvement regarding the project's time, quality/scope and/or cost. The latter dimensions constitute the "iron

Table 1 Impact of collaborative initiatives in the Antwerp cluster

Activities in the value chain	Time	Improvement of quality/scope	Cost
Primary activities			
Inbound logistics	D	D	D
Operations	A, B	A, B	A
Outbound logistics	D	D	D
Marketing and sales			
Service	B	B	
Supporting activities			
Infrastructure	B	B	B
HRM	A, B, E, F	A, B, E, F, H	A, B, E, F, H
Technology development	A, C	A, C	A, C
Procurement		G	G

triangle" in project management literature. They are used to evaluate a project's success (Atkinson 1999; Jugdev and Müller 2005). Later studies extended these dimensions (Jugdev and Müller 2005) by adapting them to a project's specificities. However, we still consider the three original dimensions to be the three basic project success factors.

Project A: Wastewater Treatment

In 1979, after having been accused of polluting the river Scheldt, VIBNA ordered a study about the river's water quality. The study contradicted the accusations. In addition, it pointed at the huge differences between the cluster firms regarding their wastewater quality. Consequently, poorer performing firms became aware of their deficiency and started taking initiatives to improve. They consulted with the better performing cluster firms. This way they bundled the existing cluster firms' expertise, resulting in improved individual and joint performances. Thus, collaboration between the cluster firms improved the solution's quality and scope. Furthermore it raised awareness for the problem, generating a quicker response and leading to a more cost-effective solution. Looking at the value chain, wastewater treatment technology was exchanged and improved, resulting in greener firm operations. Also the firms' employees were trained quicker and more cost-efficient because of this information exchange.

Project B: Safety and Environment in Operations

VIBNA continually sought safety and environmental improvements in the firms' operations. Therefore, employees had regular meetings in VIBNA's safety working groups and environmental working groups to exchange experience and skills. This caused a huge learning effect. Because of these regular meetings, managers had more and more informal contacts. In case of a problem, a safety manager will ask advice from the other cluster firms' experts by a quick telephone call. Some examples of joint projects are the uniformization of emergency signals and of subcontractors' work permits to curtail safety risks. The collaboration contributed to safety quality and raised awareness for much more safety issues. Consequently, the firms took care of these issues much sooner than when they had no support from the other cluster firms. In some cases, this also resulted in a cost advantage, e.g., in the case of employee training. Also the quality and time needed for subcontractors' planning and control (i.e., "service" in the value chain) were positively influenced due to collaboration.

Project C: Waste Processing

In 1985 the government issued a ban to dump any more waste products at the Hooge Maey dumping site. VIBNA, in close consultation with the government and some other actors involved, was one of the organizations spurring the foundation of Indaver, a waste processing firm. Because VIBNA represented a large number of important firms, they succeeded in convincing the Flemish government to participate financially. Thus, collaboration resulted in reduced costs and a quick and joint solution for the waste problem. In addition, the firms shared their expertise in waste processing. Each firm put a number of experts at Indaver's disposal. Prior to their job at Indaver, the waste processing firm's top managers have always gained expertise in one of the cluster's chemical firms.

Project D: Logistics

The cluster firms did not collaborate explicitly around logistics. However, indirect collaboration took place via the logistics firm Katoennatie. Solvay was the first cluster firm that collaborated with

Katoennatie. At the time, this was unusual, as all cluster firms used to take care of their own logistics. The project was successful; both partners benefited because of mutual learning, resulting in more efficient and more effective inbound and outbound logistics. Also logistics speed was positively influenced. Later on, other cluster firms also started collaborative projects with Katoennatie. This way, they profited from Katoennatie's knowledge and experience, gained during their partnership with Solvay. Katoennatie experienced a strong growth, becoming an important partner for a large number of cluster firms. Although no explicit collaboration took place, the firms profited from being located in the cluster; they benefited from the partner's expertise, gained during their partnership with other cluster firms.

Project E: Employee Training
The firms of the petrochemical and chemical cluster jointly organize regular safety trainings for their employees. Also governmental service providers (fire brigade, police, etc.) are involved. The main goals are to jointly elaborate and/or improve emergency plans and to train employees to create a safer working environment. The firms organize a simulation of an industrial accident at one firm site. Other firms are invited as observers. Afterward, the simulation is jointly evaluated to maximize learning. Here, collaboration results in more efficient and more effective employee training. In addition, more experience is gained during a shorter time span than in the case of individual safety trainings. Also the governmental service providers experience an increased learning effect. Through the firms' collaboration, only one single safety training has to be undertaken for all firms.

Project F: The ACTA Project
The ACTA project is an initiative of SIRA to train each year about 25 juveniles to become process operators via a part-time studying and part-time working trajectory. The project does not have a direct environmental impact. However, it results in new employees already trained for the specific safety issues of the petrochemical and chemical firms. Therefore, this project contributes to the quality, speed, and cost efficiency of the employees' safety training.

Project G: Safety Equipment

Safety is an extremely important issue in the cluster; it can have a huge impact on employees, the local community, and the environment. Therefore, safety investments are substantial. A small part of these investments consist of safety equipment, such as safety masks and suits. In exceptional circumstances, the need for safety equipment can be huge. This would mean that every single firm should require a very large stock of safety equipment in case such an exceptional circumstance takes place. However, the cluster firms agreed that in the event of such an exceptional circumstance in one of the cluster firms, they can make use of each other's safety equipment. This means that the stocks of safety equipment can be reduced to a level that is sufficient for the large majority of possible incidents. This results in a reduction of costs, as well as in an improvement of quality, i.e., access to an extremely large stock of safety equipment if needed.

Project H: I-Bus

In 2009 six cluster firms, in collaboration with VOKA, introduced a joint employee transportation plan. 3000 employees are transported more efficiently to and from their workplace. This results in economic and ecological gains. The total number of busses diminished from 53 before the project to 41 after the joint initiative. At the same time, more stops are served.

7 Discussion and Conclusions

This paper looks into environmental collaboration in clusters. The concept of clusters is not unequivocal. The most cited definition is from Porter (2000), containing three important elements: firms active in the same or in related industries, geographical proximity, and vertical or horizontal links between the firms. Clusters generate a number of advantages. They increase productivity, stimulate innovation, and attract new firms (Porter 1998, 2000). Advantages stemming from a cluster's collaborative initiatives can be called cluster-specific advantages.

In a cluster, the firms create a joint resource base by sharing resources (Verbeke and Vanden Bussche 2005; Dyer and Singh 1998). This resource base is often located in a cluster organization that coordinates and facilitates the cooperative initiatives. Hart's (1995) natural resource-based view suggests that these resources can generate green capabilities that may result in a cluster-specific advantage.

We performed a case study of the petrochemical and chemical cluster in the Antwerp port to illustrate a cluster's contribution to firms' environmental strategies. Therefore, we identified a large number of cluster organizations and discussed their importance, especially related to environmental matters. The study shows the multitude of contacts between those organizations and between the cluster's individual actors. In addition, it shows the large number of collaborative initiatives. Some cluster organizations have a large direct impact on the cluster firms, while others, especially those with a broader geographical sphere of influence, only have an indirect impact. The cluster's collaboration on environmental issues is mainly coordinated by a small number of local cluster organizations, i.e., VIBNA, SIRA, and VOKA Grootindustrie and one regional organization Essenscia Flanders.

This paper described a number of collaborative projects in the cluster. They prove the cluster's advantages, in terms of time, quality, scope, and cost, for almost all value chain activities of the firms. A lot of projects imply a bundling of knowledge and expertise, creating a win-win situation for all firms and allowing them to obtain a competitive advantage relative to firms outside the cluster. Cluster membership allows a firm to get access to the cluster's joint knowledge base, whether it is via a cluster organization or via a joint partner which has acquired its expertise during partnerships with other cluster members.

We could still observe a number of complexities that had not been described in cluster literature to date. Future research should focus on the existence of several cluster categories and their divergent characteristics. The role of governments throughout clusters' life cycles should be examined further in light of the existence of several cluster categories and its impact of the possibilities for collaboration.

References

Atkinson, R. (1999). Project management: Cost, time and quality, two best guesses and a phenomenon, it's time to accept other success criteria. *International Journal of Project Management, 17*(6), 337–342.

Audretsch, D. B. (1987). An empirical test of the industry life cycle. *Weltwirtschaftliches Archiv, 123*(2), 297–308.

Barney, J. (1991). Firm resources and sustained competitive advantage. *Journal of Management, 17,* 99–120.

Bergman, E. M. (2006). The sustainability of clusters and regions at Austria's accession edge. In Zbigniew Bochniarz & Gary B. Cohen (Eds.), *The environment and sustainable development in the New Central Europe*. New York: Berghahn.

Bergman, E. M. (2008). Cluster life-cycles: An emerging synthesis. In C. Karlsson (Ed.), *Handbook of research on cluster theory* (pp. 114–132). Northampton, MA: Edward Elgar.

Bleischwitz, R., & Thomas, L. (2007). Networks, decision-making of companies and evaluation: Concepts and terminology. In *Corporate governance of sustainability: A co-evolutionary view on resource management* (pp. 83–96). Cheltenham: Elgar.

Carroll, A. B. (1999). Corporate social responsibility: Evolution of a definitional construct. *Business and Society, 38*(3), 268–295.

Decarolis, D. M., & Deeds, D. L. (1999). The impact of stocks and flows of organizational knowledge on firm performance: An empirical investigation of the biotechnology industry. *Strategic Management Journal, 20,* 953–968.

Dyer, J. H., & Singh, H. (1998). The relational view: Cooperative strategy and sources of interorganizational competitive advantage. *Academy of Management Review, 23,* 660–679.

Esty, D. C., & Porter, M. E. (2002). Ranking national environmental regulation and performance: A leading indicator of future competitiveness? In K. Schwab, M. E. Porter, & J. D. Sachs (Eds.), *The global competitiveness report 2001–2002* (pp. 78–100). New York: Oxford University Press.

Fernhaber, S. A., Gilbert, B. A., & McDougall, P. P. (2003). *The impact of geographic location on the internationalization of new ventures*. Paper Presented at the Babson Kauffman Entrepreneurship Research Conference, Boston, 5–8 June 2003.

Folta, T. B., Cooper, A. C., & Baik, Y. (2006). Geographic cluster size and firm performance. *Journal of Business Venturing, 21,* 217–242.

Grabher, G. (1993). *The embedded firm*. London: Routledge.
Hart, S. L. (1995). A natural-resource-based view of the firm. *Academy of Management Review, 20,* 986–1014.
Hassink, R., & Shin, D. H. (2005). South Korea's shipbuilding industry: From a couple of cathedrals in the desert to an innovative cluster. *Asian Journal of Technology Innovation, 13*(2), 133–155.
Hoen, A. (2001). *Clusters: Determinants and effects*. CPB Memorandum, CPB Netherlands Bureau for Economic Policy Analysis. http://www.cpb.nl/sites/default/files/publicaties/download/memo17.pdf. Accessed on April 1, 2013.
Jans, T., Verbeke, A., & Haezendonck, E. (2015). The impact of inter-firm cooperation on proactive environmental strategies of firms: A resource-based meso-perspective (Working Paper).
Jugdev, K., & Müller, R. (2005). Success is a moving target: A retrospective look at project success and our evolving understanding of the concept. *Project Management Institute, 36*(4), 19–31.
Kamer van Koophandel Antwerpen-Waasland. (2003). *Routeplan: In stroomversnelling naar 2012*, s.l., s.n.
Kreukels, A. M. J., & Wever, E. (1998). *North Sea ports in transition: Changing tides*. Assen, The Netherlands: Van Gorcum.
Krugman, P. (1991). Increasing returns and economic geography. *Journal of Political Economy, 99,* 483–499.
Lamote, S. (2013). *Het federale en Vlaamse aankoopbeleid in emissierechten*, s.l., 11.11.11.
Lavie, D. (2006). The competitive advantage of interconnected firms: An extension of the resource-based view. *Academy of Management Journal, 31,* 638–658.
Maggioni, M. A. (2004). *Rise and fall of industrial clusters: Technology and the life cycle of regions*. Documents de treball IEB, 6.
Marshall, A. (1920). *Principles of economics*. London: Macmillan.
Martin, R., & Sunley, P. (2006). Path dependence and regional economic evolution. *Journal of Economic Geography, 6*(4), 395–437.
Maskell, P., & Kebir, L. (2005). *What qualfies as a cluster theory?* Danish Research Unit for Industrial Dynamics 9, 5–9 (Working Paper).
Maskell, P., & Lorenzen, M. (2004). The cluster as market organisation. *Urban Studies, 41*(5–6), 991–1009.
McEvily, B., & Zaheer, A. (1999). Bridging ties: A source of firm heterogenity in competitive capabilities. *Strategic Management Journal, 20,* 1133–1156.

Menzel, M. P., & Fornahl, D. (2010). Cluster life cycles: Dimensions and rationales of cluster evolution. *Industrial and Corporate Change, 19*: 205–238.
Muizer, A., & Hospers, G. J. (2000). *SMEs in regional industry clusters.* Zoetermeer: EIM.
Orsenigo, L. (2001). The (failed) development of a biotechnology cluster: The case of Lombardy. *Small Business Economics, 17,* 77–92.
Port of Antwerp. 2005. *Annual report.* Antwerp: Port of Antwerp.
Porter, M. E. (1998). Clusters and the new economics of competition. *Harvard Business Review, 76*(6), 77–90.
Porter, M. E. (2000). Location, competition, and economic development: Local clusters in a global economy. *Economic Development Quarterly, 14,* 15–34.
Porter, M. E., & Van der Linde, C. (1995). Toward a new conception of the environment-competitiveness relationship. *Journal of Economic Perspectives, 9*(4), 97–118.
Prahalad, C. K., & Hamel, G. (1990). The core competence of the corporation. *Harvard Business Review, 68*(3), 79–91.
Roh, H. S. (2007). *Port cluster systems: Supporting port logistics processes.* Seoul: Jongkum.
Rugman, A. M., & Verbeke, A. (2001). Subsidiary-specific advantages in multinational enterprises. *Strategic Management Journal, 22*(3), 237–250.
Sainsbury, D. (1999). *Biotechnology clusters.* Department of Trade and Industry.
Sharma, S., & Vredenburg, H. (1998). Proactive corporate environmental strategy and the development of competitively valuable organizational capabilities. *Strategic Management Journal, 19,* 729–753.
Su, Y. S., & Hung, L. C. (2009). Spontaneous vs. policy-driven: The origin and evolution of the biotechnology cluster. *Technological Forecasting and Social Change, 76*(5), 608–619.
Swann, G. M. P. (2002). Towards a model of clustering in high-technology industries. In G. M. P. Swann, M. Prevezer, & D. Stout (Eds.), *The dynamics of industrial clustering.* Oxford: Oxford University Press.
Tappi, D. (2005). Clusters, adaptation and extroversion: A cognitive and entrepreneurial analysis of the marche music cluster. *European Urban and Regional Studies, 12*(3), 289–307.
Uzzi, B. (1996, August). The sources and consequences of embeddedness for the economic performance of organizations: The network effect. *American sociological review, 61*(4), 674–698.

Van Klink, A., & De Langen, P. (2001). Cycles in industrial clusters: The case of the shipbuilding industry in the Northern Netherlands. *Tijdschrift voor economische en sociale geografie, 92*(4), 449–463.

Verbeke, A., & Vanden Bussche, S. (2005). Regional and global strategies in the intercontinental passenger airline industry: The rise of alliance specific advantages. In A. Verbeke (Ed.), *Internalization, international diversification and the multinational enterprise: Essays in honour of Alan M. Rugman.* Oxford: Elsevier.

Verbeke, A., Bowen, F., & Sellers, M. (2006). *Corporate environmental strategy: Extending the natural resource-based view of the firm.* Paper Presented at the annual meeting of the Academy of Management, Atlanta.

Wolter, K. (2003). *A life cycle for clusters? The dynamics governing regional agglomerations.* Paper Presented at Conference: Clusters, Industrial Districts and Firms: The Challenge of Globalization, Modena.

Zack, M. H. (1999). Managing codified knowledge. *Sloan Management Review, 40,* 45–58.

6

The Impact of Collaboration on Green Competitive Advantage in Europe's Largest Petrochemical Cluster

Tim Jans, Elvira Haezendonck and Alain Verbeke

1 Introduction

A large number of studies have looked into the impact of a firm's localization in a geographical cluster. In one of the most well known, Porter (1998) explained that fierce competition within a cluster

T. Jans
Vrije Universiteit Brussel (VUB), Brussels, Belgium

E. Haezendonck (✉)
Department of Business, Vrije Universiteit Brussel (VUB), Brussels, Belgium
e-mail: elvira.haezendonck@vub.be

A. Verbeke
Haskayne School of Business, University of Calgary, Calgary, AB, Canada
e-mail: alain.verbeke@haskayne.ucalgary.ca

Department of Business, Vrije Universiteit Brussel, Brussels, Belgium

Henley Business School, University of Reading, Reading, UK

E. Haezendonck and A. Verbeke (eds.), *Sustainable Port Clusters and Economic Development*, Palgrave Studies in Maritime Economics,
https://doi.org/10.1007/978-3-319-96658-8_6

improves cluster firms' performance. Folta et al. (2006) looked at the impact of cluster size on cluster firms' innovation rate, alliance partners, and private investors. They found increasing individual performances until the cluster consisted of about 65 firms, after which the effect reversed. Decarolis and Deeds (1999) observed a positive link between cluster membership and the firm's financial performance. Clusters are mostly considered as fruitful environments to generate competitive advantage because they increase productivity, stimulate innovation, and attract new firms (Porter 1998, 2000; Marshall 1920). Other advantages of cluster membership are an increased likelihood that the firm internationalizes and, hence, results in higher international sales (Fernhaber et al. 2003). However, Porter (1998) indicated that a cluster needs at least ten years to establish a certain depth and create a competitive advantage, indicating that potentially not all benefits are immediately and automatically generated. Many researched positive impacts of clusters at least suggest that the cooperation of multiple firms in a geographical area stimulates some form of collaboration or synergy. Little attention, as also recently pointed out by Wassmer et al. (2014) in the context of environmental collaborations in particular, has been given to the causal effects and mediating factors of collaborations leading to green firm benefits.

Managers would however benefit from more insight into how the positive effects are generated and the processes that lead to the cluster firms' advantages. It can help to understand how to use the cluster's network to their advantage, making their firms more competitive compared to firms outside the cluster's network and supporting decisions as from membership considerations up to cluster-specific investments. Furthermore and specifically related to socioeconomic issues, such as environmental impacts, understanding the processes that lead to an increase of environmental investments which go beyond compliance, and making firms more competitive at the same time, is also valuable information for policymakers. They might become more aware of the specific stimuli that can trigger and/or reinforce a firm's (voluntary) efforts for the natural environment and may as such be more supportive of clusters or other forms of collaboration.

Wassmer et al. (2012) did an extensive literature study of all forms of environmental collaborations and discussed antecedents and consequences of these collaborations. This paper has a strong focus on inter-firm collaborations and concludes that inter-firm collaborations for environmental issues "can be seen as vehicles to realize economic value through addressing environmental problems" (Wassmer et al. 2012: 6).

The current paper builds on this and analyzes how specifically the cluster affects its firms' environmental strategies and the extent to which this results in competitive advantage. We start by looking at whether the cluster can increase the cluster firms' environmental investments and environmental performance, after which we study how these investments may lead to a competitive advantage for the cluster firms. Such a potential advantage will indeed create economic value, but at the same time may increase public benefits in such a way that these exceed the benefits firms can generate on their own.

The next section of this paper explains the underlying theoretical basis of the paper and formulates hypotheses which will be empirically tested. The third section explains the methodology used to obtain the results showed in section four. The fifth section of this paper discusses the results and formulates conclusions.

2 Theory and Hypotheses

2.1 Theoretical Framework

We build our analysis in this paper on an extension of the natural resource-based view (Verbeke et al. 2006; based on Hart 1995). The resource-based view describes how firms can obtain a sustained competitive advantage with their resources and their capabilities resulting from these resources (Barney 1991; Grant 1991). Resources are "the tangible and intangible assets a firm uses to choose and implement its strategies" (Barney 2001: 54). This definition implies that a firm does not necessarily need to own or control the resources. Therefore, we can extend the resource-based view to analyze inter-firm collaborative initiatives or systems in which the firms operate as a higher-level unit within which resources are shared. These shared resources are termed network resources (McEvily and Zaheer 1999; Lavie 2006). McEvily and Zaheer (1999) showed empirically, by using the resource-based view as theoretical framework, that networks, such as a cluster of firms, make a valuable contribution to the development or range of competitive advantages of a firm. Network resources may as such constitute an additional source of competences. The idea of shared resources is also used in Dyer and Singh's (1998) "relational view." However, they argue that "at a fundamental level, relational rents are possible when alliance partners combine, exchange, or invest in idiosyncratic assets, knowledge, and resources/capabilities, and/or they employ effective governance mechanisms that lower transaction costs or permit the realization of rents through the synergistic combination of assets, knowledge, or capabilities" (Dyer and Singh 1998: 662). Parise and Casher (2003) introduced the idea of looking at inter-firm relations, in their case alliance relationships, as a portfolio of business partners to be managed with the goal of achieving greater business success. Wassmer and Dussauge (2011: 60) studied alliance portfolios taking a resource-based perspective. They find that "an important issue for the focal firm [is] to deal with [...] the fit of a network resource with both its own resources as well as other network resources accessed from partners of other alliances." All these contributions share the idea that inter-firm relations through a network or alliance relationship could definitely increase the potential of business success or even greater competitive advantage.

Hart (1995) was the first to explicitly link environmental strategies and the resource-based view of the firm, which he termed the "natural resource-based view of the firm." He stated that firms can achieve a competitive advantage by developing competencies with their resources that foster eco-friendly activities. This hypothesis has since been empirically validated by among others (Sharma and Vredenburg 1998; Verbeke et al. 2006). We build upon the extended resource-based view (McEvily and Zaheer 1999; Lavie 2006) and the natural resource-based view (Hart 1995) and more specifically extend the Verbeke et al. (2006) approach to empirically analyze the impact of the largest European petrochemical cluster on the green competitive advantage of the cluster's firms. We argue that firms in this cluster create a joint resource base out of which all participating organizations can tap knowledge and other necessary and useful resources for supporting environmental strategies. These resources are added to the firm's own resource base and are an additional source for the development of competencies that foster eco-friendly activities.

The type of network we will use in this study is the network in a geographical cluster. We identified several cluster theories in the existing cluster literature. The two most cited theories are from Porter (2000) and Krugman (1991) (Hoen 2001; Roh 2007). Porter (2000) regards clusters as geographically proximate organizations in the same or in related sectors, linked by vertical or horizontal relations. Krugman (1991) indicated the wider macro-oriented socioeconomic benefits clusters may have. Because Porter (2000) considered clusters from a more microeconomic perspective, as *"geographic concentrations of interconnected companies, specialized suppliers, service providers, firms in related industries, and associated institutions (e.g., universities, standards agencies, trade associations) in a particular field that compete but also cooperate"* (Porter 2000: 15). Building upon Wassmer and Dussauge's (2012) work about alliance portfolios, we may argue that a geographical cluster is a portfolio of business partners and competitors. It is up to the cluster firms to utilize this portfolio to its full potential. At least, the cluster environment stimulates firms to combine network resources with both their own resources to increase their business success and to create competitive advantage.

2.2 Hypotheses

Buysse and Verbeke (2003) identified five environmental resource domains in Hart's (1995) work in which a company can invest to improve its resource base internally. By investing in these resource domains, the firm will augment its capacity for developing competencies that foster eco-friendly activities. Based on Hart's (1995) natural resource-based view, these competencies may lead to a competitive advantage. The resource domains identified are: (1) conventional green competencies related to green product and manufacturing technologies, (2) employee skills, (3) organizational competencies, (4) formal (routine-based) management systems and procedures, at the input, process, and output sides, and (5) the reconfiguration of the strategic planning process (Buysse and Verbeke 2003).

A number of authors have described various internal organization drivers for environmental investments or environmental initiatives within the organization, i.e., drivers of investments in one or more of the five resource domains. Among the most discussed factors are the individual preferences and values of upper echelon managers, resulting in an eco-centric leadership style. Cordano and Frieze (2000) found that environmental managers' attitude toward pollution prevention is positively related to the preference for implementation of these activities. This attitude and the consequent response might be formed by the manager's individual concern, i.e., "*the degree to which [they] value the environment and the degree of discretion they possess to act on their environmental values*" (Bansal and Roth 2000). Eco-centric leadership causes "*faster diffusion and tighter integration of environmental values [...] and leads to a higher degree of formalization of environmental responsibilities within the organization*" (Branzei et al. 2004: 1088). Furthermore, eco-centric leaders also succeed in finding support from others in the organization for their strategic decisions (Branzei et al. 2004). Finally, eco-centric leadership occurs more often when there is organizational slack, i.e., an excess of resources available to managers (Sharma 2000; Bansal 2003).

A second internal organization factor influencing environmental investments is the managerial interpretation of environmental issues as opportunities instead of threats. Sharma (2000) found that the greater the degree to which a manager interprets environmental issues as opportunities, the greater the likelihood of choosing for a proactive environmental strategy. On the other hand, interpreting environmental issues as threats causes a manager to rather choose for a reactive environmental strategy.

The third factor is championing by environmental managers. Championing consists of three activities: "*(1) identifying/generating an issue or idea, (2) packaging it as attractive, and (3) selling it to organizational decision makers*" (Andersson and Bateman 2000: 549). The main reason that a manager might become an environmental champion is out of individual concerns. To be successful, it also has to be an issue in line with the organization's values, so as to be perceived as strategically important (Bansal 2003).

The last factor is supervisory behavioral support. These are all actions and behaviors from upper echelon managers that might positively influence environmental initiatives from employees. This can be in the form of a well-defined and well-communicated environmental policy, i.e., an organizational encouragement, but even more important are supervisor encouragement supporting innovation, competence building, and communication with others (Ramus and Steger 2000). Also the use of rewards and recognition and assisting in managing goals and responsibilities were found to be important supervisory behavioral support factors that can result in more investments in the five environmental resource domains. Cordano and Frieze (2000) hypothesized that more hierarchical control of environmental managers would lead to better pollution prevention results, but they could not find a significant result for this relationship. On the contrary, they found significant results in the opposite direction. This could suggest that a too strict hierarchical control, limiting the actions or innovative decisions of an environmental manager, might have a reverse effect on the environmental performance.

As the natural resource-based view suggests, investing in the five resource domains stimulates the development of eco-friendly firm-specific capabilities (Verbeke et al. 2006; Hart 1995). Sharma and Vredenburg (1998) identified three organizational capabilities emerging from environmental investments: stakeholder integration, higher-order learning, and continuous innovation. In our study, we focus on stakeholder integration and higher-order learning, because continuous innovation, as also suggested by Sharma and Vredenburg (1998) and Verbeke et al. (2006), is already integrated in or at least overlapping with the capability for higher-order learning.

Stakeholder integration "*involves the ability to establish trust-based collaborative relationships with a wide variety of stakeholders, especially those with noneconomic goals. These stakeholders may include local communities, environmental groups, regulators, non-governmental organizations (NGOs),* etc." (Sharma and Vredenburg 1998: 735). Maxwell et al. (1997) explain that managers' decision about which strategy to pursue is dependent on market factors and non-market factors. Thus, when a manager chooses for a strategy involving collaboration, this choice might be based on economic and noneconomic motives and result in collaboration with market and non-market stakeholders (Baron 1995). Collaboration with market stakeholders intends to enhance a firm's competitive position. Related to environmental strategies, this implies the use of a green strategy to obtain a competitive advantage relative to competitors (Maxwell et al. 1997; Hart 1995; Sharma and Vredenburg 1998). Also a better financial performance (Douglas and Judge 1995; Hart and Ahuja 1996; Murphy 2002), an increased operational performance (Hart and Ahuja 1996), and higher stock prices or a higher market value of the firm (Klassen and McLaughlin 1996; Dowell et al. 2000) are market factors driving firms to proactive environmental strategies. While collaboration with market stakeholders serves to increase a firm's economic performance, collaboration with non-market stakeholders is more suited to increase a firm's overall performance (Baron 1995), including the environmental performance (Maxwell et al. 1997).

"*Higher-order learning involves the development of different interpretations of new and existing information, as a result of developing new understandings of surrounding events*" (Sharma and Vredenburg 1998: 740; Fiol 1994). It is a form of organizational learning, allowed, stimulated, and enhanced by four contextual factors: the extent to which the corporate culture is suited for enhancing learning, the extent to which it allows flexibility, the extent to which the organizational structure allows innovation, and, finally, the environment (Fiol and Lyles 1985).

The natural resource-based view (Hart 1995) further explains that when a firm develops eco-friendly capabilities due to its investments in the five resource domains, some of the capabilities might result in a sustainable competitive advantage for the firm, if they are valuable, rare, non-imitable, and non-substitutable (Barney 1991). We distinguish three dimensions of green competitive advantage: a cost advantage, a product differentiation advantage, and the reinforcement of the firm's future market position (Sharma and Vredenburg 1998; Verbeke et al. 2006). Cost reduction is aimed at lowering inputs and/or increasing outputs. Product differentiation involves both new product development and improvements of existing products. Finally, reinforcement of the firm's future market position entails making the firm more competitive in terms of employees' learning skills, the firm's reputation, its customer satisfaction, and its market share (Verbeke et al. 2006).

Based on the extended natural resource-based view (Barney 1991; Grant 1991; Hart 1995; McEvily and Zaheer 1999; Lavie 2006), we find support that in a lot of cases, at least some of the investments in the five resource domains are stimulated, facilitated, or increased by the networks in which the firm participates, i.e., in this case the geographical cluster network. Verbeke and Vanden Bussche (2005: 127) explained that an alliance's knowledge base depends upon the synergies that result from resources of various partners through an evolutionary process. Similar to this, a cluster's resource base can be enhanced by collaboration. In other words, the cluster may stimulate the investments in the five resource domains. As these investments are determined by internal organization drivers, the cluster network may enhance the effect of the internal organization drivers, causing an increased effect on the investments in the five resource domains.

Hypothesis 1a: *The internal drivers of proactive environmental investments are reinforced by cluster collaboration.*

Hypothesis 1b: *The cluster-induced part of each internal driver of proactive environmental strategies leads to investments in the five resource domains.*

Hypothesis 2a: *Investments in the five environmental resource domains increase due to cluster collaboration.*

Consequently, the use of the extended natural resource-based model of Verbeke et al. (2006) in this paper suggests that also the development of eco-friendly firm-specific capabilities is enhanced by cluster collaboration, and that the cluster-induced part of the investments in the five resource domains also contributes to the development of eco-friendly firm-specific capabilities. Although the shared resources alone might make a significant contribution, it will also be the unique combination of firm-specific with cluster-specific resources that will make a large contribution to the development of these capabilities.

Hypothesis 2b: *Cluster-induced investments in the five resource domains lead to the development of firm-specific capabilities.*

Hypothesis 3a: *Firm-specific capabilities can be enhanced through cluster collaboration.*

As the natural resource-based view (Hart 1995) explains, these capabilities might result in superior, sustainable firm-specific advantage. As this will in theory be the case for all the firms participating in the cluster, we could speak of a cluster-specific competitive advantage. However, due to the combination with each firm's own resources and capabilities, this advantage will be different for each firm.

Hypothesis 3b: *Cluster-induced firm-specific capabilities may lead to a firm-specific competitive advantage.*

Hypothesis 4: *Firm-specific competitive advantage can be enhanced through cluster collaboration.*

3 Method

3.1 Data and Sample

The sample for this study consists of firms in the petrochemical and chemical cluster of Antwerp and Rotterdam. Because of the geographical proximity (less than 100 km), the intense pipeline network and many (supply chain) relations between both sub-clusters, Antwerp and Rotterdam, are at least for (petro)chemicals in a global competitive context, considered as one cluster, being the most important one in Europe. Next to the (petro)chemical industry, the cluster involves related industries, as mentioned in Porter's (2000) cluster definition, such as oil refining and cracking firms, tank storage firms, transport firms, and construction and maintenance firms. In addition to the firms active in the cluster for this paper's quantitative analysis, we have interviewed the main responsible of four cluster organizations in Antwerp and two in Rotterdam, to obtain additional qualitative information. Based on their activities and location in the cluster, we identified 161 firms. For the Antwerp part of the cluster, we selected based on a yearly publication listing all the relevant firms located in the Antwerp port area (De Lloyd 2010), 70 in total. For the cluster part in Rotterdam, we built our respondents list based on information provided by the Rotterdam Port Authority (2010) as well as Deltalinqs information, a local interest group for the Rotterdam port area, which finally resulted in 91 firms for the Rotterdam part of the cluster. We contacted all the 161 firms by phone and asked for a face-to-face semi-structured interview with the environmental manager or the plant manager on their site. This resulted in 59 in-depth interviews (response rate 36, 7%) conducted in a period of eight months from June 2010 until February 2011.

3.2 Survey Design and Measures

A survey was developed and was a basic part of and for the conducted half-structured interviews. Besides an in-depth discussion of each question, all questions were finally answered in written together with the respondents and each interview took on average about one hour and a half. The survey used in Verbeke et al. (2006) was used as a basis, but was updated with items from more recent literature and extended with relevant cluster items. Verbeke et al. (2006) survey items were based upon empirical literature contributions from 1995 to 2005. Industry experts and academic experts assessed face (content) validity of the summated scales of the survey, and the authors incorporated the experts' feedback into the survey instrument. We checked more recent literature up until 2012 and literature up until 2005 that had not been included in their list of references. A list of 101 possible new items or adaptations of existing items were composed and discussed in our team of authors. We concluded that with some minor adaptations and extensions to the existing item list, all new items were covered in our survey. Table 1 shows the list of concepts and items integrated in the survey. Items that

Table 1 Rating scales

Eco-centric leadership (Branzei et al. 2004)

1. Many of our senior managers are personally and actively involved in developing environmental protection policies for our firm
2. Many of our senior managers are personally and actively involved in monitoring the implementation of environmental protection policies for our firm
3. Our senior managers give environmental issues a high priority
4. Ideas on pollution management are shared freely among lower, middle, and upper levels within my organization
5. Most people in my organization are very aware of the need to protect the environment
6. Most people in my organization are well informed about our environmental policy

Interpretation of environmental issues as opportunities

1. Investments in environmental initiatives could translate into opportunities or benefits for the business (Bansal and Roth 2000)
2. There are more opportunities for our business arising out of the environmental agenda than threats (Sharma et al. 1999)
3. Our environmental agenda provides us with unique business opportunities that are not generated by other activities (Verbeke et al. 2006)
4. Our environmental manager regularly urges us to view our environmental agenda a as business opportunity (Sharma et al. 1999)
5. I or other managers are likely to lose rather than gaining by initiating actions to preserve the environment (Sharma 2000)
6. Any action that I or other managers may take for environmental preservation is constrained by others in the organization (Sharma 2000)
7. I am confident that I have best practice knowledge to reduce the environmental impact of company operations (Sharma 2000)

Championing of environmental managers (Cordano and Frieze 2000)

Our environmental manager thinks that:

1. Pollution prevention is the most desirable waste management goal
2. Most pollution prevention projects are worthwhile
3. Pollution prevention is an important component of a company's environmental management
4. Pollution prevention should be seen as an important component of a company's "bottom line"

Lower-level support

1. Employee suggestions have proven to be an excellent source of ideas to improve environmental performance for the company (Klassen and Whybark 1999)
2. The company has demonstrated its support to rank and file employees' new ideas (Ramus and Steger 2000)

(continued)

Table 1 (continued)

Higher-order learning (Sharma and Vredenburg 1998)
My company is able to:
1. Generate cooperation among line-staff to exchange environmental information and the integration of such information
2. Continuously expand knowledge about the business/natural environment interface
3. Look for solutions to environmental problems from fresh angles
4. Act before the rest of the industry
5. Preempt regulations
6. Experiment on the business/natural environmental domain
7. Spot opportunities amidst changes in social expectations and environmental regulations
8. Innovate and continuously improve operations while reducing environmental impact
Stakeholder integration
This item is measured differently, as explained in this paper. The four items measuring this concept in Verbeke et al. (2006) survey are dropped
Cost reduction (Sharma and Vredenburg 1998)
My company's proactive environmental practices have helped my company to be more competitive in terms of:
1. Lower material costs
2. Lower process/production costs
3. Lower costs of regulatory compliance
4. Increased productivity
5. Process innovations
6. Increased knowledge about effective ways of managing operations
Product differentiation (Sharma and Vredenburg 1998)
1. Product innovation
2. Improved product quality
Securing of the future market position (Sharma and Vredenburg 1998)
1. Organization-wide learning among employees
2. Improved employee morale
3. Overall improved company reputation or goodwill
4. Customer satisfaction
5. Market leadership

(continued)

Table 1 (continued)

Resource domain 1 (Sharma and Vredenburg 1998)
1. Implementing processes that reduce/eliminate the production of pollutants
2. Continuously improving pollution prevention results
3. Disposing of and treating hazardous/toxic wastes
4. Implementing pollution/emission control equipment
5. Recycling
6. Using waste produced as input somewhere else
7. Implementing control/alarm systems for environmental accidents
8. Observing rigorous emergency response procedures
9. Insurance planning to cover potential environmental risks
10. Carbon capture and storage
Resource domain 2
1. Training or educating employees on environmental issues (Sharma and Vredenburg 1998)
Realigning employee responsibilities to allow them adequate time to:
2. Receive environmental training (Ramus and Steger 2000)
3. Explore new environmental techniques (Ramus and Steger 2000)
4. Visit sites (Ramus and Steger 2000)
Resource domain 3
1. Coordinating the environmental efforts of various functional areas within the organization (Verbeke et al. 2006)
Improving environmental performance through greener:
2. Purchasing of production equipment (Douglas and Judge 1995; Buysse and Verbeke 2003)
3. Production (Sharma and Vredenburg 1998)
4. Distribution (wholesale and retail) (Sharma and Vredenburg 1998; Buysse and Verbeke 2003)
5. Supply chain management (Sharma and Vredenburg 1998; Buysse and Verbeke 2003)
6. R&D (Buysse and Verbeke 2003)
7. Legal and policy functions (Douglas and Judge 1995)
8. Public relations (e.g., attracting environmental conscious investors/customers) (Douglas and Judge 1995)
One item from Verbeke, Bowen, and Sellers (2006) has been dropped, i.e., "improving environmental performance through greener refining," as this is an item too specific for the oil industry, and in addition, this item is overlapping with the item "improving environmental performance through greener production"

(continued)

Table 1 (continued)

Resource domain 3
1. Coordinating the environmental efforts of various functional areas within the organization (Verbeke et al. 2006)
Improving environmental performance through greener:
2. Purchasing of production equipment (Douglas and Judge 1995; Buysse and Verbeke 2003)
3. Production (Sharma and Vredenburg 1998)
4. Distribution (wholesale and retail) (Sharma and Vredenburg 1998; Buysse and Verbeke 2003)
5. Supply chain management (Sharma and Vredenburg 1998; Buysse and Verbeke 2003)
6. R&D (Buysse and Verbeke 2003)
7. Legal and policy functions (Douglas and Judge 1995)
8. Public relations (e.g., attracting environmental conscious investors/customers) (Douglas and Judge 1995)
One item from Verbeke et al. (2006) has been dropped, i.e., "improving environmental performance through greener refining," as this is an item too specific for the oil industry, and in addition, this item is overlapping with the item "improving environmental performance through greener production"
Resource domain 4
1. Using formal procedures to review environmental concerns for all new capital investments for the company (Klassen and Whybark 1999)
2. Publishing a formal, well-defined environmental policy (Buysse and Verbeke 2003; Ramus and Steger 2000)
3. Setting specific targets for environmental performance (Ramus and Steger 2000)
4. Conducting environmental Life Cycle Assessment on major products (Sharma and Vredenburg 1998; Ramus and Steger 2000; Buysse and Verbeke 2003)
5. Implementing an Environmental Management System (Bansal and Roth 2000; Ramus and Steger 2000)
6. Publishing audit results of waste production programs annually for production areas (Sharma and Vredenburg)
7. Reviewing operating practices for their impact on the environment (Bansal and Roth 2000)
8. Publishing environmental reports (Buysse and Verbeke 2003; Ramus and Steger 2000)
9. Selection of cleaner logistics methods (González-Benito and González-Benito 2005)
10. Environmental criteria in supplier selection (González-Benito and González-Benito 2005)

(continued)

Table 1 (continued)

Resource domain 5
1. My organization has an environmental officer at the senior management level (Branzei et al. 2004)
2. Environmental managers or those chiefly responsible for environmental management in my organization have adequate authority over capital investment decisions (Branzei et al. 2004)
3. Reports of environmental performance are sent to management or directors (Buysse and Verbeke 2003)
4. Environmental reports are used actively by senior management (Buysse and Verbeke 2003)
5. Our senior managers are aware of company-specific environmental issues (Bansal and Roth 2000)
6. Our business plan includes an extensive, detailed section that describes the company's objectives for environmental performance (Klassen and Whybark 1999; Sharma 2000)
7. Reviewing environmental concerns (Klassen and Whybark 1999)
8. Environmental strategic planning (Buysse and Verbeke 2003)
9. Identifying and evaluating emerging environmental issues for their long-term (five years or more) impact on the company (Klassen and Whybark 1999)

are underlined have been adapted or added. If items were dropped from Verbeke, Bowen, and Sellers' survey, this is mentioned in the table. We extended the list of items to be measured because our survey also tries to assess the cluster impact on a list of concepts.

Most questions were measured on a seven-point Likert scale (1 = "strongly disagree" or "no importance," 7 = "strongly agree" or "strong importance"). For each measured item, we also asked whether the respondent believed that due to the effects of the cluster, there has been a positive effect on the answer given for the item. If yes, we asked whether this effect was caused by information exchange in the cluster, or whether the effect was obtained by means of a specific joint project with one or more other cluster firms. In the latter case, we also asked if the respondent's firm was the leading or one of the leading firms in the project. For all items measuring the investments in the five resource domains (except for the first six items of resource domain 5), we also asked whether the firm is investing in the item topic for at least five years to check whether it is a sustained investment. To measure the concept of stakeholder integration, we used a method already applied by several previous authors (Buysse and Verbeke 2003; Henriques and

Sadorsky 1999; Sharma and Henriques 2005; Rueda-Manzanares et al. 2008), namely:

$$\text{Stakeholder integration} = \sum_i \mu_i \beta_i$$

where: μ_i = the interest of this stakeholder in environmental issues;
β_i = the level of attention the firm pays to this stakeholder.

We selected 19 stakeholder groups to measure stakeholder integration, i.e., (1) domestic customers, (2) international customers, (3) domestic suppliers, (4) international suppliers, (5) employees, (6) labor unions, (7) shareholders, (8) financial institutions, (9) domestic rivals, (10) international rivals, (11) international agreements, (12) ENGOs, (13) media, (14) national governments, (15) regional governments, (16) provincial governments, (17) local public agencies (e.g., municipal authority), (18) port authority, and (19) local community groups. We also measured the extent to which cluster stakeholders were taken into account by asking for the importance and active involvement in a number of local cluster organizations. These organizations were identified based on preliminary interviews with a number of cluster organizations. Finally, a number of control variables were included: plant size (measured as the natural logarithm of the number of full time equivalents), location/seaport area (Antwerp or Rotterdam), and industry (i.e., oil/chemical industry or other industry).

4 Analysis

First, we compute the scores of the pre-defined concepts based on the respondents' answers. We check for internal consistency with Cronbach's alpha. If this value is acceptable, we compute each respondent's concept score by averaging the item scores. For the items measuring investments in the resource domains, the score is reset to 1 (i.e., the investment has no importance in terms of investments made, managerial time devoted, or general commitment of the organization) if the investment is non-sustainable. In accordance with Verbeke et al. (2006), an investment is considered to be not sustained when it is not done for at least the last five years. For each concept, we compute a general score and a cluster-induced score. For the internal organization drivers for example, we measured whether the cluster has an effect on these internal organization drivers. For example, to measure the internal organization driver "eco-centric leadership," we asked, among other questions, whether the firm's senior managers gave environmental issues a high priority. Next, we discussed with the respondent whether the cluster has contributed to this, i.e., whether their senior managers would have given a lower priority to environmental issues in the absence of the cluster. If so, we discussed with the respondent whether the effect was due to an information exchange with one or more cluster partners. Information exchange is the simplest form of cluster collaboration, in which no joint projects are done, but in which information that can help other cluster firms is exchanged. When the firm had one or more specific joint projects with other cluster firms, the intensity of cluster collaboration is larger. In our example, senior managers may have given a higher priority to environmental issues because, e.g., another firm in the joint project has highlighted the importance of the environmental topic, or just because due to the project, they became more aware of it. The strongest type of collaboration observed is collaboration in the form of projects in which the interviewed firm plays a leading role. The cluster-induced score reflects the presence of the internal organization driver and the extent to which the cluster had contributed to this presence. The score is 1 when the cluster has had no contribution (i.e., there is no cluster collaboration for this item) or when the internal organization driver is absent. On the other hand, the score is 7 when there is a very strong presence of the internal organization driver of proactive environmental strategies, and when the cluster has contributed very strongly to this presence (i.e., there are joint projects for this item, in which this firm plays a leading role). The item scores are computed by multiplying the item scores for the presence of each internal organization driver with their respective scores for the cluster contribution (0 = no cluster contribution, 1 = information exchange, 2 = joint project (no lead), and 3 = joint project as lead firm). Next, the cluster-induced concept scores are computed analogously to the concept scores. These scores are then rescaled to a scale from 1 to 7. We chose not to standardize the data, as this would efface the difference between the normal scores' averages and the cluster-induced scores' averages. Furthermore, it would efface the difference in standard deviations. For stakeholder integration, the cluster-induced score is computed differently. We had to measure a score reflecting somehow the "cluster integration." Contrary to the regular score for stakeholder integration, we only took into account the cluster organizations as stakeholders here, as we try to measure to cluster-induced part of stakeholder integration. In other words, cluster-induced stakeholder integration measures the additional stakeholder integration due to the relations and contacts with and within the cluster organizations. We first identified the local cluster organizations in each part of the cluster (i.e., five cluster organizations for Antwerp and four for Rotterdam). We asked for the importance of each organization regarding environmental issues and the extent to which the firms are actively involved in the cluster organization. The remaining steps are analogously with the normal score for stakeholder integration.

Hypotheses 1a, 2a, 3a, and 4 are tested by means of *t*-tests. The cluster-induced variables have a score from 1 (no cluster contribution) to 7 (the variable score is very high and the cluster contribution to this high score is very strong). We test whether the score is significantly larger than 1 to determine whether the cluster has an impact. Hypotheses 1b, 2b, and 3b are tested by means of linear regression analyses.

As a number of variables are dependent on one another, we expect some correlation problems (see Table 2). However, a variable is never used in an analysis in combination with its cluster-induced variant. Furthermore, we think that the high correlation between the cluster-induced variables is due to the general effect of the cluster on a firm, i.e., the cluster effect on a firm causes a similar effect on all this firm's variables. Multicollinearity is therefore a problem when we estimate the joint effect of the independent variables on the dependent variable. However, we decided to always include the independent variables in separate models one at a time. This way, we estimate the impact of each cluster-induced internal organization driver of environmental investments on the investments in each resource domain separately. Furthermore, the effects of the cluster-induced investments in each resource domain on the development of stakeholder integration and higher-order learning are estimated. However, we also estimate the

Table 2 Descriptive statistics and correlations table

	Variable	Mean	SD	Items	α	1	2	3	4	5	6	7	8	9	10	11	12	13	14
1.	Eco-centric leadership	5.59	0.86	6	.793														
2.	Managerial interpretation	4.98	0.95	7	.689	.52**													
3.	Championing of environmental managers	5.75	1.00	4	.780	.47**	.46**												
4.	Supervisory behavioral support	4.86	1.30	2	†	.25	.31*	.12											
5.	Investments in RD1	4.18	1.42	10	.844	.15	.33*	−.05	.25										
6.	Investments in RD2	3.83	1.56	4	.733	.18	.30*	−.03	.41**	.76**									
7.	Investments in RD3	3.20	1.62	8	.866	.04	.22	−.14	.18	.72**	.63**								
8.	Investments in RD4	3.75	1.71	10	.893	.01	.17	−.10	.10	.71**	.66**	.75**							
9.	Investments in RD5	5.13	1.27	9	.824	.11	.20	−.02	.19	.72**	.61**	.68**	.76**						
10.	Higher-order learning	5.02	1.03	8	.883	.65**	.67**	.42**	.34**	.39**	.37**	.29*	.19	.31*					
11.	Stakeholder integration	4.92	1.06	††	/	.22	.18	.22	.08	.11	.12	.13	.17	.26*	.31*				
12.	Lower costs	4.53	1.40	6	.884	.42**	.37**	.16	.47**	.24	.35**	.34*	.23	.02	.44**	.06			
13.	Product differentiation	4.29	1.77	2	†	.39**	.27*	.13	.39**	.19	.27*	.33*	.16	.03	.33*	.05	.66**		
14.	Securing future position	4.83	1.48	5	.933	.55**	.37**	.29*	.51**	.22	.34*	.15	.06	.13	.47**	.17	.72**	.70**	
15.	Cluster-induced eco-centric leadership	2.70	0.68	6		.57**	.41**	.22	.38**	.25	.26	.33*	.14	.16	.49**	.28*	.43**	.36**	.40**
16.	Cluster-induced managerial interpretation	2.45	0.65	7		.35**	.64**	.15	.33*	.41**	.38**	.38**	.28*	.29*	.60**	.25	.42**	.31*	.34**
17.	Cluster-induced championing	2.83	0.80	4		.16	.29*	.37**	.21	.06	.09	.17	.02	−.01	.22	.15	.29*	.29*	.24
18.	Cluster-induced supervisory behavioral support	2.25	0.71	2		.05	.14	−.11	.65**	.31*	.33*	.32*	.16	.18	.24	.05	.32*	.28*	.29*

(continued)

Table 2 (continued)

	Variable	Mean	SD	Items	α	1	2	3	4	5	6	7	8	9	10	11	12	13	14
19.	Cluster-induced investments in RD1	2.61	0.91	10		.28*	.30*	−.04	.25	.65**	.54**	.66**	.50**	.44**	.39**	.09	.41**	.41**	.30*
20.	Cluster-induced investments in RD2	2.27	0.90	4		.15	.25	−.01	.26*	.54**	.71**	.57**	.48**	.43**	.24	−.08	.24	.29*	.30*
21.	Cluster-induced investments in RD3	2.24	0.75	8		.14	.14	−.04	.11	.40**	.37**	.67**	.47**	.46**	.17	.23	.31*	.39**	.32*
22.	Cluster-induced investments in RD4	2.18	0.77	10		−.03	.04	−.12	.06	.50**	.48**	.54**	.75**	.54**	.07	.09	.18	.20	.15
23.	Cluster-induced investments in RD5	2.57	1.21	9		.06	.09	−.11	.22	.43**	.32*	.44**	.30*	.30*	.21	.11	.17	.22	.12
24.	Cluster-induced higher-order learning	2.71	0.92	8		.42**	.44**	.01	.33*	.45**	.39**	.45**	.33*	.39**	.65**	.16	.46**	.37**	.36**
25.	Cluster-induced stakeholder integration			††		.19	.19	−.09	.20	.40**	.34**	.26*	.39**	.38**	.32*	.38**	.20	.03	.22
26.	Cluster-induced lower costs	2.40	0.89	6		.29*	.34*	.16	.35**	.27*	.26*	.44**	.29*	.17	.40**	.05	.76**	.50**	.50**
27.	Cluster-induced product differentiation	2.22	1.02	2		.14	.28*	−.09	.26	.24	.24	.33*	.19	−.02	.30*	.13	.49**	.74**	.44**
28.	Cluster-induced securing of future position	2.30	0.76	5		.47**	.48**	.21	.46**	.33*	.36**	.36**	.19	.19	.56**	.27*	.65**	.62**	.73**
29.	Plant size	4.46	1.70			.02	−.10	−.12	.05	.26*	.24	.14	.25	.25	.03	−.09	.08	−.03	−.03
30.	Seaport	0.59				.12	.18	.08	.15	.15	.11	.13	−.03	.01	.13	.14	.27*	.19	.28*
31.	Activity in oil or chemical industry	0.47				.02	.06	−.11	.16	.43**	.36**	.43**	.61**	.47**	.04	.09	.20	.08	.01

(continued)

Table 2 (continued)

	15	16	17	18	19	20	21	22	23	24	25	26	27	28	29	30
...																
16.	.69**															
17.	.52**	.57**														
18.	.55**	.55**	.33*													
19.	.58**	.65**	.41**	.44**												
20.	.39**	.53**	.38**	.41**	.69**											
21.	.39**	.42**	.48**	.24	.71**	.54**										
22.	.18	.33*	.34**	.20	.60**	.56**	.68**									
23.	.53**	.43**	.33*	.45**	.48**	.39**	.35**	.35**								
24.	.55**	.74**	.33*	.53**	.70**	.45**	.45**	.35**	.31*							
25.	.32*	.41**	0.12	.35**	.45**	0.12	.27*	.35**	.39**	.45**						
26.	.59**	.59**	.45**	.44**	.58**	.35**	.52**	.32*	.32*	.60**	.20					
27.	.44**	.48**	.32*	.46**	.48**	.29*	.37**	.24	.30*	.46**	.27*	.55**				
28.	.64**	.68**	.44**	.55**	.58**	.45**	.50**	.29*	.31*	.67**	.34*	.72**	.66**			
29.	−.10	.02	−.27*	.00	.13	.13	−.09	.08	−.05	.15	.15	.02	−.21	−.14		
30.	.15	.15	.08	.11	.25	.18	.17	−.09	.18	.26	.01	.28*	.16	.37**	.12	
31.	.14	.24	.00	.19	.42**	.27*	.30*	.42**	.24	.23	.35**	.29*	.13	.12	.23	.10

*Correlation is significant at the 0.05 level (2-tailed)

**Correlation is significant at the 0.01 level (2-tailed)

†These constructs only contain two items, so Cronbach's alpha is not computed. For Supervisory behavioral support, $r=0.273$, $p=0.040$. For product differentiation, $r=0.752$, $p=0.000$

††Stakeholder integration is measured differently

impact of simultaneous investments in the five resource domains on the development of these capabilities, but these results have to be interpreted more carefully due to the problem of multicollinearity. Finally, we estimate the impact of the cluster-induced capabilities for stakeholder integration and for higher-order learning on each dimension of competitive advantage. Again, the simultaneous as well as the separate impact is estimated. In each analysis, we have to be aware that the separate models are much more trustworthy because here the independents are not impacted by multicollinearity. Therefore, conclusions will be based on the separate models. Next, as the dependent and independent variables are measured by the same instrument, there is a possibility for common method bias. Also consistency bias, occurring when respondents try to avoid contradictory attitudes, perceptions, or attributions in their self-reported responses, could have impacted our data (Staw 1975). However, we believe that due to the fact that the surveys were completed by means of face-to-face interviews conducted by one person only, namely the first author, we believe that the impact of this type of bias was minimized. The same is valid for acquiescence bias, the tendency to always agree with the questions. When the interviewer detected acquiescence bias, more background information about the questions was asked to check whether the respondents were answering in accordance with their real opinions, attitudes, or perceptions. Finally, we tried to limit social desirability bias, the tendency to give socially acceptable answers, by guaranteeing that the answers are confidential, and that no individual results are communicated or published.

5 Results

Hypotheses 1a, 2a, 3a, and 4 are tested by means of one-tailed *t*-tests. The variables, calculated with observed scores, are scored from 1 (no cluster contribution) to 7 (the variable score is very high, and the cluster contribution to this high score is very strong). In other words, we have to test whether the scores are significantly larger than 1.

The results are shown in Table 3. Hypothesis 1a tests whether the cluster-induced internal drivers of proactive environmental strategies,

Table 3 One-tailed *t*-tests to test for cluster contribution (test value = 1)

Variable	Mean	SD	*t*	*p*-value
Cluster-induced eco-centric leadership	1.87	0.76	8.78	.000
Cluster-induced managerial interpretation of environmental issues as opportunities	1.73	0.69	8.08	.000
Cluster-induced championing by environmental managers	2.00	0.96	7.87	.000
Cluster-induced supervisory behavioral support	1.50	0.74	5.20	.000
Cluster-induced investments in RD1	1.98	0.95	7.91	.000
Cluster-induced investments in RD2	1.75	0.89	6.47	.000
Cluster-induced investments in RD3	1.66	0.69	7.20	.000
Cluster-induced investments in RD4	1.56	0.67	6.41	.000
Cluster-induced investments in RD5	1.55	0.56	7.64	.000
Cluster-induced higher-order learning	1.97	0.83	9.01	.000
Cluster-induced stakeholder integration[a]	2.43	1.13	9.77	.000
Cluster-induced cost reduction	1.79	0.87	6.81	.000
Cluster-induced product differentiation	1.63	1.00	4.63	.000
Cluster-induced securing of the future market position	1.58	0.73	6.00	.000

[a]The score for cluster-induced stakeholder integration is computed differently from the other cluster-induced concept scores

i.e., eco-centric leadership, managerial interpretation of environmental issues as opportunities, championing by environmental managers and supervisory behavioral support, do exist. All four cluster-induced internal drivers are significantly larger than 1, so hypothesis 1a is supported. Hypothesis 2a tests whether the investments in the five resource domains are enhanced by the cluster. This is the case for all five resource domains, so also hypothesis 2a is supported. Hypothesis 3a tests whether the cluster-induced capabilities developed from the investments in the five resource domains, i.e., stakeholder integration and higher-order learning, exist. Both capabilities have scores significantly larger than 1, so the analysis supports hypothesis 3a. Finally, hypothesis 4 tests whether there is a cluster contribution to the development of sustainable competitive advantage. All three dimensions of cluster-induced competitive advantage are significantly larger than 1, so also hypothesis 4 is supported.

Hypotheses 1b, 2b, and 3b are tested by means of linear regression analyses. Hypothesis 1b tests whether the cluster-induced part of internal drivers of proactive environmental strategies (i.e., cluster-induced eco-centric leadership, cluster-induced managerial interpretation of environmental issues as opportunities, cluster-induced championing by environmental managers, and cluster-induced supervisory behavioral support) leads to investments in the five resource domains. This hypothesis is tested for each resource domain. The results are shown in Table 4.

In model 1, only the control variables are added to the model. Model 2 adds the independent variables. The independent testing variables have correlations ranging between .33 and .69. However, as explained above we base our conclusions on the models 3–6. Table 4, resource domain 1, shows that the investments in conventional green competencies related to green product and manufacturing technologies, i.e., resource domain 1, are positively influenced by the cluster-induced impact of eco-centric leadership and by the cluster-induced impact of the managerial interpretation of environmental issues as opportunities. The other two internal organization drivers of environmental proactivity do not have an effect on the investments resource domain 1. For resource domain 2, i.e., investments in employee skills, Table 6.4 shows that we can make an identical conclusion: cluster-induced eco-centric leadership and cluster-induced managerial interpretation of environmental issues as opportunities have a positive impact on the investments in employee skills, while the other two internal organization drivers of environmental investments have not. The results for the impact of the internal organization drivers of environmental proactivity on the investments in resource domain 3, the organizational competencies, are also shown in Table 4. Models 3 to 6 show that all four internal organization drivers of environmental proactivity have a significantly positive impact on the investments in organizational competencies. However, as shown in Table 4, investments in resource domain 4, i.e., in formal (routine-based) management systems and procedures, at the input, process, and output sides, are not influenced by the cluster-induced internal organization drivers of environmental proactivity. This last conclusion is also valid for investments in resource domain 5, the reconfiguration of the strategic planning process. In sum, hypothesis 1b is partly supported.

Table 4 Results of the linear regression analyses for hypothesis 1b

Independent variables	Dependent variable	Resource domain 1						Resource domain 2					
	Description / Model	1	2	3	4	5	6	1	2	3	4	5	6
PS	Plant size	.099	.112	.162	.104	.101	.113	.222	.258	.294†	.227	.224	.234
SP	Seaport	.433	.334	.312	.353	.422	.393	.205	.078	.065	.130	.191	.169
OCH	Activity in oil or chemicals	.924*	.610†	.805*	.670†	.910*	.852**	.830*	.540	.[illegible]93†	.594	.814†	.766†
ECO	Cluster-induced eco-centric leadership		.071	.413†					.244	.476†			
OPP	Cluster-induced managerial interpretation of environmental issues as opportunities		.877*		.690**				.701		.643*		
CHA	Cluster-induced championing by environmental managers		−.247			.135			−.199			.163	
SUP	Cluster-induced supervisory behavioral support		−.021				.346		−.086				.309
Constant		3.088**	2.113*	2.136*	2.044**	2.824**	2.554**	2.278**	1.176	1.181	1.305	1.962*	1.801*
R^2		.193*	.317**	.240**	.299**	.202*	.228**	.151*	.235†	.139*	.222*	.161†	.173*
p of R^2		.010	.007	.007	.001	.019	.009	.035	.061	.021	.011	.057	.043
ΔR^2 (model 1)			.124†	.046†	.106**	.009	.035		.083	.047†	.071*	.010	.021
p of ΔR^2			.086	.085	.008	.450	.137		.281	.039	.036	.438	.258

Independent variables	Resource domain 3						Resource domain 4						Resource domain 5					
	1	2	3	4	5	6	1	2	3	4	5	6	1	2	3	4	5	6
PS	.344*	.442**	.460**	.339*	.339*	.355*	.327*	.359*	.374*	.329*	.328*	.332*	.150	.152	.1[illegible]4	.153	.150	.153
SP	.267	.038	.022	.182	.234	.205	−.361	−.451	−.452	−.404	−.369	−.377	.019	−.027	−.027	−.019	.019	.012
OCH	.956*	.688†	.715†	.690†	.917*	.845*	1.723**	1.553**	1.633**	1.588**	1.713**	1.694**	.878**	.704*	.8[illegible]2**	.759*	.877**	.865**
ECO		.685†	.833**					.239	.313					.047	.1[illegible]8			
OPP		.138		.723*				.378		.367				.585		.323		
CHA		.022			.381†			−.114			.101			−.206			.005	
SUP		.079				.535*		−.126				.141		−.163				.061
Constant	1.048	−.906	−.871	−.045	.307	.222	1.621*	.916	.900	1.065	1.424†	1.402†	4.077**	3.737**	3.[illegible]13**	3.589**	4.067**	3.983**
R^2	.241**	.384**	.380**	.327**	.294**	.302**	.398**	.425**	.416**	.418**	.401**	.402**	.211**	.267*	.2[illegible]0*	.243**	.211*	.213*
p of R^2	.002	.001	.000	.000	.001	.001	.000	.000	.000	.000	.000	.000	.006	.029	.0[illegible]2	.006	.015	.014
ΔR^2 (model 1)		.143	.139**	.086*	.053†	.061*		.027	.018	.020	.003	.004		.056	.0[illegible]9	.032	.000	.001
p of ΔR^2		.037	.001	.014	.056	.039		.687	.218	.188	.592	.567		.466	.4[illegible]9	.150	.972	.760

*$p<.05$
**$p<.01$
†$p<.10$

Hypothesis 2b states that the cluster-induced investments in the five resource domains lead to the development of firm-specific capabilities, i.e., a capability for stakeholder integration and a capability for higher-order learning. The analysis is repeated for each capability. The results are shown in Table 5. Correlations between the independent testing variables range between .35 and .71, causing multicollinearity in the models 2 in Table 5. In addition, the total number of variables in the analysis is rather large for our data set. Therefore, our conclusions are based on models 3–7, in which the individual impact of the cluster-induced investments in each resource domain is tested for its impact on the development of a capability for stakeholder integration and for higher-order learning.

Table 5 shows that the cluster-induced investments in the five resource domains do not have an effect on the development of a capability for stakeholder integration. On the other hand, a capability for higher-order learning is developed due to the cluster-induced investments in resource domains 1 and 2. The cluster-induced investments in the resource domains 3–5 have no effect on the development of this capability, either. Hypothesis 2b is partly supported.

Finally, hypothesis 3b states that the cluster-induced firm-specific capabilities may lead to a firm-specific competitive advantage. The analyses are shown in Table 6.

Correlation between the variables cluster-induced stakeholder integration and cluster-induced higher-order learning is .45. However, we decided again to base our conclusions on the models 3 and 4. Table 6 shows the results of the regressions estimating the impact of the cluster-induced development of the two capabilities on cost reduction. The results show that cluster-induced higher-order learning indeed leads to cost reduction, while the cluster-induced capability for stakeholder integration does not. Also product differentiation is positively impacted by a cluster-induced capability for higher-order learning, but not by cluster-induced stakeholder integration, as shown in Table 6. Finally, Table 6 shows that cluster-induced higher-order learning is not adequate for the securing of the firm's future position. Here, the cluster-induced capability for stakeholder integration has a significant impact on this dimension of competitive advantage. In sum, each dimension of competitive advantage is enforced by one of the cluster-induced capabilities, so hypothesis 3b is supported.

An outline of the results is visualized in Fig. 1.

Table 5 Results of the linear regression analyses for hypothesis 2b

Independent variables	Dependent variable	Stakeholder integration							Higher-order learning						
	Description / **Model**	1	2	3	4	5	6	7	1	2	3	4	5	6	7
PS	Plant size	−.070	.000	−.066	−.034	−.090	−.079	−.075	−.063	−.075	−.100	−.106	−.093	−.079	−.067
SP	Seaport	.328	.268	.345	.405	.273	.338	.305	.203	−.036	.067	.113	.118	.219	.180
OCH	Activity in oil or chemicals	.209	.200	.243	.259	.153	.188	.145	.186	−.033	−.088	.127	.100	.147	.124
CRD1	Cluster-induced investments in RD 1		−.052	−.053						.432†	.427**				
CRD2	Cluster-induced investments in RD 2		−.463†		−.261					.048		.306†			
CRD3	Cluster-induced investments in RD 3		.441			.220				.150			.336		
CRD4	Cluster-induced investments in RD 4		−.384				.068			−.353				.123	
CRD5	Cluster-induced investments in RD 5		.596					.277		.018					.263
Constant		4.957**	4.497**	5.014**	5.163**	4.746**	4.900**	4.592**	5.154**	4.780**	4.694**	4.912**	4.833**	5.050**	4.807**
R^2		.034	.173	.036	.073	.051	.035	.054	.020	.170	.151†	.080	.065	.025	.040
p of R^2		.601	.289	.746	.406	.593	.751	.571	.780	.303	.070	.352	.468	.856	.706
ΔR^2 (model 1)			.139	.002	.039	.017	.001	.019		.150	.131**	.060†	.045	.005	.020
p of ΔR^2			.175	.760	.148	.338	.797	.307		.145	.007	.072	.120	.622	.305

*$p<.05$
**$p<.01$
$^{\dagger}p<.10$

Table 6 Results of the linear regression analyses for hypothesis 3b

Independent variables	Dependent variable	Cost reduction				Product differentiation				Securing future market position			
	Description / Model	Model 1	Model 2	Model 3	Model 4	Model 1	Model 2	Model 3	Model 4	Model 1	Model 2	Model 3	Model 4
PS	Plant size	−.069	−.062	−.070	−.061	−.047	−.021	−.047	−.031	−.127	−.126	−.130	−.122
SP	Seaport	.748†	.556	.748†	.548	.670	.435	.670	.466	.889*	.798†	.888*	.744†
OCH	Activity in oil or chemicals	.535	.325	.398	.345	.246	.156	.268	.038	.052	−.223	−.189	−.085
CSI	Cluster-induced stakeholder integration		.037	.181			−.243	−.006			.250	.317†	
CHL	Cluster-induced higher-order learning		.475†		.496*		.710*		.565†		.222		.358
Constant		4.151**	3.301**	3.782**	3.344**	3.983**	3.238**	3.995**	3.020**	4.890**	4.020**	4.244**	4.307**
R^2		.106	.186†	.125	.185*	.041	.124	.041	.106	.089	.152	.140†	.125
p of R^2		.111	.056	.131	.029	.549	.258	.718	.229	.174	.125	.092	.132
ΔR^2 (model 1)			.079†	.019	.079*		.083	.000	.065†		.063	.051†	.036
p of ΔR^2			.094	.294	.029		.115	.980	.064		.161	.084	.147

*$p<.05$
**$p<.01$
$^{\dagger}p<.10$

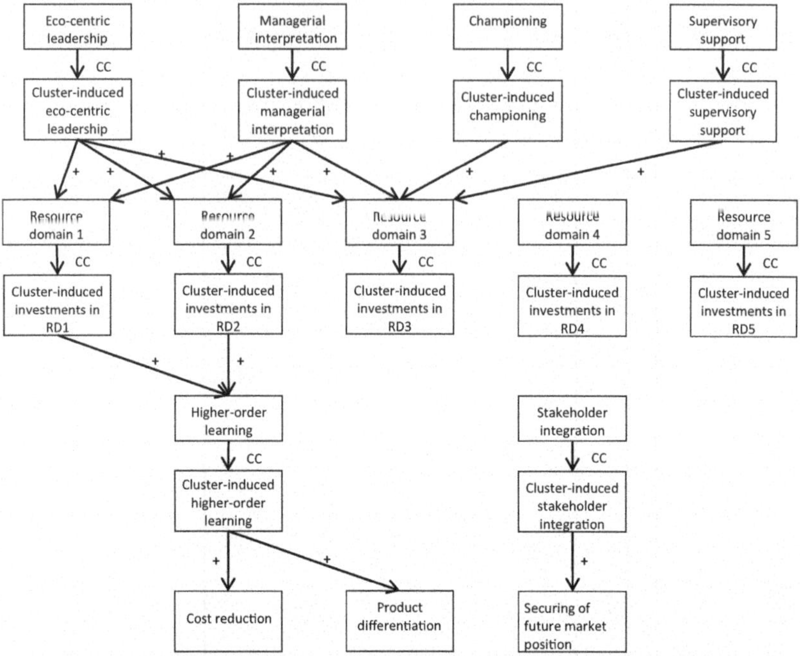

Fig. 1 Visualization of the analytical results (cc: Cluster collaboration; this step lifts out the part of the variable that is due to cluster collaboration. This step is only performed when we have statistically determined that the cluster-induced part exists)

6 Discussion and Conclusion

Our results show that the largest European petrochemical cluster contributes positively to the presence of internal organization drivers of proactive environmental strategies, i.e., to eco-centric leadership, to a managerial interpretation of environmental issues as opportunities, to championing by environmental managers, and to supervisory behavioral support. Thus, we can conclude that a specific part of the internal drivers of environmental investments exists due to explicit collaborative actions and initiatives from the cluster members.

We find that cluster-induced eco-centric leadership increases the investments in the resource domains 1, 2, and 3, but not in the resource domains 4 and 5. This is only partly in line with our expectations based on previous literature (Noda and Bower 1996; Bansal and Roth 2000; Cordano and Frieze 2000; Sharma 2000; Bansal 2003; Branzei et al. 2004; Verbeke et al. 2006). We could assume that eco-centric leadership which finds its origin in the cluster has the same effect as when coming from other origins. This study confirms this assumption: Cluster-induced eco-centric leadership positively impacts the investments in conventional green competencies related to green product and manufacturing technologies, investments in employee skills, and investments in organizational competencies. However, we did not find that eco-centric leadership that finds its origin in the cluster drives investments in formal (routine-based) management systems and procedures nor that it drives investments in the reconfiguration of the strategic planning process. We believe that this might be due to the fact that our sample consisted mainly of large subsidiaries, but no or few headquarters of (petro) chemical firms. Subsidiaries do not always have the responsibility to decide upon the management systems and procedures or strategic planning processes. Furthermore, we find that the cluster-induced managerial interpretation of environmental issues as opportunities has a similar effect as the cluster-induced eco-centric leadership driver, i.e., it increases the investments in the resource domains 1, 2, and 3, but we do not find an effect on the resource domains 4 and 5. In the literature, the managerial interpretation of environmental issues as opportunities has been identified as a driver of investments in the environmental resource domains (Sharma 2000; Verbeke et al. 2006). We found a positive effect of cluster-induced managerial interpretation of environmental issues as opportunities on the investments in conventional green competencies related to green product and manufacturing technologies, investments in employee skills, and investments in organizational competencies, but did not find this effect on the investments in formal (routine-based) management systems and procedures or in the reconfiguration of the strategic planning process. Again, we believe these last two resource domains are mainly determined by the headquarters, whereas the first three are predominantly the responsibility of the subsidiaries. Next, we found that cluster-induced championing by environmental managers contributes positively to investments in organizational competencies, i.e., resource domain 3. This resource domain determines the extent to which the environmental goals of the various functional areas in the organization are aligned and the extent to which these functional divisions participate in achieving the broader environmental strategy goals of the company. This coordination task is the specific responsibility of the environmental manager. If the environmental manager is an environmental champion, he or she has to negociate and convince others in the organisation, more than focusing on investments in resource domain 3. We might expect that the same is true for the resource domains 1 and 2, but the results do not confirm these expectations. We did not find a significant contribution of championing by the environmental manager on the investments in conventional green competencies related to green product and manufacturing technologies and in employee skills. An explanation might be that contrary to resource domain 3, which is almost exclusively the responsibility of the environmental manager, the investments in resource domain 1 are often to be approved by the management team, and not just the environmental manager. Some firms in our sample even needed the approval of their headquarters for these investments. An environmental manager that is an environmental champion has to negotiate and convince others in the organization more than in the case of investments in resource domain 3. The same might be true for the investments in employee skills, i.e., resource domain 2. However, an additional factor that might play is that employee training is often given during other training sessions, where environmental issues are just mentioned. Training sessions specifically for environmental matters are extremely rare. Therefore, the direct impact that the environmental champion might have on the investments in employee skills is low. He/she might impact the quality of the environmental trainings, but probably not the quantity or the exclusive attention for environmental matters. Again, due to the nature of our sample, we do not find a significant impact of championing activities by the environmental manager on the investments in the resource domains 4 and 5. Confirming what was found in the literature (Cordano and Frieze 2000; Ramus and Steger 2000; Verbeke et al. 2006) also supervisory behavioral support contributes positively to the investments in the five environmental resource domains. Although supervisory, behavioral support is impacted by the cluster, this only happens to a limited extent. In most companies, this is a purely internal matter. We only find a significant result for the investments in organizational competencies. The supervisory support, mainly aimed at involving lower echelons in generating ideas for environmental improvement, seems to be adequate for improving the coordination of environmental efforts among the various functional areas in the organization. However, supervisory behavioral support originating from the cluster collaboration is not sufficiently large (see Table 3) to have a significant impact on the investments in conventional green competencies related to green product and manufacturing technologies and in employee skills. We do not find a significant effect on the investments in the resource domains 4 and 5 either because of the nature of our sample. However, also the small effect of the cluster on supervisory behavioral support might be the cause of the absence of a significant impact.

Furthermore, our results showed that the investments in the environmental resource domains were enhanced by the cluster via information exchange or via joint projects in the cluster. Based on the extended natural resource-based view of the firm (Hart 1995; McEvily and Zaheer 1999; Lavie 2006), we expected that these enhanced investments would lead to the development of a capability for stakeholder integration and a capability for higher-order learning (Verbeke et al. 2006). However, although we find that stakeholder integration is enhanced by the cluster, we do not find evidence that this effect is due to the cluster-enhanced investments in the environmental resource domains. There may be another influencing factor which we did not include in our model, which is a weakness of our study.

Based on our research, we can state that explicit cluster collaboration increases the number of contacts between the cluster firms. Managers will come more into contact with other firms in the cluster (suppliers, customers, and competitors) as well as with noneconomic organizations such as environmental NGOs or port authorities, as these are drawn to or created for the cluster due to the geographical concentration of firms. As the number of contacts increases, also the level of stakeholder integration might increase. This might explain that we do find an impact of the cluster on stakeholder integration, but this effect does not take place via the cluster-induced investments in the environmental resource domains.

The development of a capability for higher-order learning, on the contrary, is enhanced by cluster-induced investments in resource domains 1 and 2, i.e., by cluster-induced investments in conventional green competencies related to green product and manufacturing technologies and in employee skills. These investments bring along a significant effect on the development of organizational learning related to environmental issues. However, we do not find a significant effect of cluster-induced investments in organizational competencies, in formal (routine-based) management systems and procedures and in the reconfiguration of the strategic planning process on the capability for higher-order learning. For resource domain 3, we believe that this might be due to the fact that the environmental investments in organizational competencies, i.e., the coordination of environmental goals of the various functional divisions of the organization, is mainly a responsibility of the environmental manager, so there is an insufficient impact on the "general" higher-order learning of the organization. For resource domains 4 and 5, as explained before, we believe that due to the nature of the petrochemical and chemical industry, the investment decisions are made predominantly by the headquarters. Finally, we also tested whether the cluster increases the competitive advantage of the cluster firms. We found evidence that all three dimensions of competitive advantage, i.e., cost reduction, product differentiation, and the securing of the future market position, were enhanced by the cluster. According to the extended natural resource-based view of the firm (Hart 1995; McEvily and Zaheer 1999; Lavie 2006), competitive advantage is enhanced by the cluster-induced development of stakeholder integration and higher-order learning. We find that this is indeed the case, but each dimension of competitive advantage is only supported by one of the capabilities. Cost reduction and product differentiation are enhanced by the cluster-induced development of higher-order learning, while the securing of the future market position is enhanced by the cluster-induced development of stakeholder integration. In other words, the cluster-induced capability for higher-order learning leads to a rather direct impact on the firm's performance by means of reducing the costs and broadening and improving the range of products of the firm. On the other hand, the cluster-induced capability for stakeholder integration has a more long-term impact, as it can maintain the firm's license to operate and secure the existence of the firm in the market. Thus, both cluster-induced capabilities combined result in shorter-term and longer-term competitive advantages for the firm.

Our results show that the internal drivers of environmental investments, the investments themselves, a capability for stakeholder integration and for higher-order learning, and competitive advantage are enhanced by the cluster network. We found that the investments in the resource domains 1–3 are positively influenced by the effect of the cluster on eco-centric leadership and on the managerial interpretation of environmental issues as opportunities. In addition, resource domain 3 is also enhanced by the effect of the cluster on championing of environmental managers and on supervisory behavioral support for environmental initiatives. Next, we found that the increased investments through the cluster contribute significantly to the development of a capability for higher-order learning. Finally, the results show that the effect of the cluster on stakeholder integration contributes to the securing of the future market position, and that the cluster's effect on higher-order learning reduces costs and increases product differentiation. In other words, the cluster-induced capabilities lead to a reinforcement of the firm's competitive advantage.

If the firm's top management is aware of the cluster effects and how these can contribute to better firm performance on several domains, they might be able to further strengthen this effect. A manager might, for example, search more actively opportunities for information exchange or joint projects with other cluster firms. This way, the cluster-induced effect on eco-centric leadership, on the managerial interpretation of environmental issues as opportunities, on championing by environmental managers, and on supervisory behavioral support can be larger. As our study shows, this should result in more investments in conventional green competencies related to green product and manufacturing technologies, in employee skills, and in organizational competencies. Furthermore, the cluster also contributes to the development of a capability for stakeholder integration, although this is not a result of the increased investments in the environmental resource domains. The additional development of the capability for stakeholder integration also results in an increased competitive advantage, i.e., a more secured future market position. This is a long-term benefit that will result in increased customer satisfaction and better employee morale. Furthermore, it will increase the company's reputation and goodwill. Thus, managers should seek to get involved in the cluster and involve stakeholders in their decision-making processes in order to maximize the cluster's contribution to the competitive position of the firm.

Also cluster organizations can benefit from the results of our study. As they are now more aware of the processes that lead to a better competitive position for the cluster firms, they might try to stimulate information exchange and joint projects further. They might especially focus on enforcing the internal organization drivers of environmental investments, as these are the basis for the cluster contribution to reduced costs and increased product differentiation. In other words, they should further stimulate eco-centric leadership, they should demonstrate that the environmental topic is an opportunity for a firm and not a threat, they should help the firms' environmental managers with their championing behavior, and they should try to stimulate the involvement of lower echelons in generating ideas that can benefit the firms' environmental goals and performances. To this end, the cluster organizations can stimulate collaboration and its effects by organizing meetings, seminars, and events for top managers focused on stimulating these internal organization drivers. The main goal is to create or improve the managers' vision and attitude toward environmental leadership and show the beneficial effects that this may have on the firms' competitive position.

Finally, policymakers also have a responsibility in enforcing the effect of a geographical cluster on its firms. They may intervene in and stimulate the effect of existing cluster organizations or enhance cluster collaboration via government-dependent cluster organizations such as port authorities in port clusters. We only studied mature clusters in which collaboration was already well developed. However, we believe that government subsidies for collaborative initiatives might be especially helpful in young clusters that have yet to discover the full beneficial effect of the cluster. Nonetheless, policymakers have to be aware that the cluster can help to drive firms toward a more proactive approach of their dealings with the environment, whereas the traditional law-making approach, focusing on setting targets, is mainly based on reactive behavior of the firms. Thus, we recommend that policymakers shift their attention toward stimulating proactive behavior. One way to do this is by seeking methods to stimulate the cluster collaboration, because, as shown is this study, this will lead to more environmental investments and a better competitive position at the same time.

References

Andersson, L. M., & Bateman, T. S. (2000). Individual environmental initiative: Championing natural environmental issues in U.S. business organizations. *Academy of Management Journal, 43,* 548–570. https://doi.org/10.2307/1556355.

Bansal, P. (2003). From issues to actions: The importance of individual concerns and organizational values in responding to natural environmental issues. *Organization Science, 14,* 510–527.

Bansal, P., & Roth, K. (2000). Why companies go green: A model of ecological responsiveness. *Academy of Management Journal, 43,* 717–736.

Barney, J. (1991). Firm resources and sustained competitive advantage. *Journal of Management, 17,* 99–120.

Barney, J. B. (2001). Is the resource-based "view" a useful perspective for strategic management research? Yes. *Academy of Management Review, 26,* 41–56.

Baron, D. P. (1995). Integrated strategy: Market and nonmarket components. *California Management Review, 37,* 47–65.

Branzei, O., Ursacki-Bryant, T. J., Vertinsky, I., & Zhang, W. (2004). The formation of green strategies in Chinese firms: Matching corporate environmental responses and individual principles. *Strategic Management Journal, 25,* 1075–1095.

Buysse, K., & Verbeke, A. (2003). Proactive environmental strategies: A stakeholder management perspective. *Strategic Management Journal, 24,* 453–470.

Cordano, M. C., & Frieze, I. H. (2000). Pollution reduction preferences of U.S. environmental managers: Applying Ajzen's theory of planned behavior. *Academy of Management Journal, 43,* 627–641.

De Lloyd. (2010). *Annual Port of Antwerp*. Antwerp: De Lloyd N.V.
Decarolis, D. M., & Deeds, D. L. (1999). The impact of stocks and flows of organizational knowledge on firm performance: An empirical investigation of the biotechnology industry. *Strategic Management Journal, 20,* 953–968.
Douglas, T. J., & Judge, W. Q. (1995). Integrating the natural environment into the strategic planning process: An empirical assessment. *Academy of Management Best Paper Proceedings, 1,* 475–479.
Dowell, G., Hart, S., & Yeung, B. (2000). Do corporate global environmental standards create or destroy market value? *Management Science, 46,* 1059–1074.
Dyer, J. H., & Singh, H. (1998). The relational view: Cooperative strategy and sources of interorganizational competitive advantage. *Academy of Management Review, 23,* 660–679.
Fernhaber, S. A., Gilbert, B. A., & McDougall, P. P. (2003). *The impact of geographic location on the internationalization of new ventures.* Babson Kauffman Entrepreneurship Research Conference, Boston, 5–8 June 2003.
Fiol, C. M. (1994). Consensus, diversity, and learning in organizations. *Organization Science, 5,* 403–420.
Fiol, C. M., & Lyles, M. A. (1985). Organizational learning. *Academy of Management Review, 10,* 803–816.
Folta, T. B., Cooper, A. C., & Baik, Y. (2006). Geographic cluster size and firm performance. *Journal of Business Venturing, 21,* 217–242.
González-Benito, J., & González-Benito, O. (2005). Environmental proactivity and business performance: An empirical analysis. *Omega, 33,* 1–15.
Grant, R. M. (1991). The resource-based theory of competitive advantage: Implications for strategy formulation. *California Management Review, 33,* 114–135.
Hart, S. L. (1995). A natural-resource-based view of the firm. *Academy of Management Review, 20,* 986–1014.
Hart, S. L., & Ahuja, G. (1996). Does it pay to be green? An empirical examination of the relationship between emission reduction and firm performance. *Business Strategy and the Environment, 5,* 30–37.
Henriques, I., & Sadorsky, P. (1999). The relationship between environmental commitment and managerial perceptions of stakeholder importance. *Academy of Management Journal, 42,* 87–99.
Hoen, A. (2001). *Clusters: Determinants and effects.* CPB Memorandum, CPB Netherlands Bureau for Economic Policy Analysis. http://www.cpb.nl/sites/default/files/publicaties/download/memo17.pdf. Accessed on April 1, 2013.

Klassen, R. D., & McLaughlin, C. P. (1996). The impact of environmental management on firm performance. *Management Science, 42,* 1199–1214.
Klassen, R. D., & Whybark, D. C. (1999). Environmental management in operations: The selection of environmental technologies. *Decision Sciences, 30,* 601–631.
Krugman, P. (1991). Increasing returns and economic geography. *Journal of Political Economy, 99,* 483–499.
Lavie, D. (2006). The competitive advantage of interconnected firms: An extension of the resource-based view. *Academy of Management Journal, 31,* 638–658.
Marshall, A. (1920). *Principles of economics.* London: Macmillan.
Maxwell, J., Rotherberg, S., Briscoe, F., & Marcus, A. (1997). Green schemes: Corporate environmental strategies and their implementation. *California Management Review, 39,* 118–134.
McEvily, B., & Zaheer, A. (1999). Bridging ties: A source of firm heterogenity in competitive capabilities. *Strategic Management Journal, 20,* 1133–1156.
Murphy, C. J. (2002). *The profitable correlation between environmental and financial performance: A review of the research.* Seattle, WA: Light Green Advisors.
Noda, T., & Bower, J. L. (1996). Strategy making as iterated processes of resource allocation. *Strategic Management Journal, 17,* 159–192.
Parise, S., & Casher, A. (2003). Alliance portfolios: Designing and managing your network of business-partner relationships. *Academy of Management Executive, 17,* 25–39.
Port of Rotterdam. (2010). *Facts & figures Rotterdam energy port and petrochemical cluster.* Rotterdam: Port of Rotterdam Authority.
Porter, M. E. (1998). Clusters and the new economics of competition. *Harvard Business Review, 76,* 77–90.
Porter, M. E. (2000). Location, competition, and economic development: Local clusters in a global economy. *Economic Development Quarterly, 14,* 15–34.
Ramus, C. A., & Steger, U. (2000). The roles of supervisory support behaviors and evironmental policy in employee "Eco initiatives" at leading-edge European companies. *Academy of Management Journal, 43,* 605–626.
Roh, H. S. (2007). *Port cluster systems: Supporting port logistics processes.* Seoul: Jongkum.
Rueda-Manzanares, A., Aragón-Correa, J. A., & Sharma, S. (2008). The Influence of stakeholders on the environmental strategy of service firms: The moderating effects of complexity, uncertainty and munificence. *British Journal of Management, 19,* 185–203.

Sharma, S. (2000). Managerial interpretations and organizational context as predictors of corporate choice of environmental strategy. *Academy of Management Journal, 43,* 681–697.
Sharma, S., & Henriques, I. (2005). Stakeholder influences on sustainability practices in the Canadian forest products industry. *Strategic Management Journal, 26,* 159–180.
Sharma, S., & Vredenburg, H. (1998). Proactive corporate environmental strategy and the development of competitively valuable organizational capabilities. *Strategic Management Journal, 19,* 729–753.
Sharma, S., Pablo, A., & Vredenburg, H. (1999). Corporate environmental responsiveness strategies: The importance of issue interpretation and organizational context. *Journal of Applied Behavioral Science, 35,* 87–108.
Staw, B. M. (1975). Attribution of the "causes" of performance: A general alternative interpretation of cross-sectional research on organizations. *Organizational Behavior and Human Performance, 13,* 414–432.
Verbeke, A., Bowen, F., & Sellers, M. (2006). Corporate environmental strategy: Extending the natural resource-based view of the firm. *Academy of Management Best Paper Proceedings, 1,* A1–A6.
Verbeke, A., & Vanden Bussche, S. (2005). Regional and global strategies in the intercontinental passenger airline industry: The rise of alliance specific advantages. In A. Verbeke (Ed.), *Internalization, international diversification and the multinational enterprise: Essays in honour of Alan M. Rugman.* Oxford: Elsevier.
Wassmer, U., & Dussauge, P. (2011). Value creation in alliance portfolios: The benefits and costs of network resource interdependencies. *European Management Review, 8,* 47–64. https://doi.org/10.1111/j.1740-4762.2011.01003.x.
Wassmer, U., & Dussauge, P. (2012). Network resource stocks and flows: How do alliance portfolios affect the value of new alliance formations? *Strategic Management Journal, 33*(7), 871–883.
Wassmer, U., Paquin, R., & Sharma, S. (2012). The engagement of firms in environmental collaborations: Existing contributions and future directions. *Business and Society, 52,* 1–33.
Wassmer, U., Paquin, R., & Sharma, S. (2014). The engagement of firms in environmental collaborations: Existing contributions and future directions. *Business & Society, 53*(6), 754–786.

Index

E. Haezendonck and A. Verbeke (eds.), *Sustainable Port Clusters and Economic Development*, Palgrave Studies in Maritime Economics,
https://doi.org/10.1007/978-3-319-96658-8

The manufacturer's authorised representative in the EU is Springer Nature Customer Service Centre GmbH, Europaplatz 3, 69115 Heidelberg, Germany. If you have any concerns regarding our products, please contact ProductSafety@springernature.com

Printed and bound by CPI Group (UK) Ltd, Croydon, CR0 4YY

30/09/2026

02225434-0001